Rob.t R. Livingston Esq.r
of Clermont

# LIFE
# ALONG
# THE
# HUDSON

# LIFE
# ALONG
# THE
# HUDSON

## THE HISTORIC
## COUNTRY ESTATES
## *of the*
## LIVINGSTON FAMILY

Written and Photographed by
PIETER ESTERSOHN

Foreword by
JOHN WINTHROP ALDRICH

*RIZZOLI*
NEW YORK

New York · Paris · London · Milan

TO MY PARENTS, CARL AND BETTY, WHO
VISITED MANY LEGENDARY HOUSES AND GARDENS
WITH ME DURING MY CHILDHOOD,
AND TO MY SON, ELIO, WITH WHOM I AM
CONTINUING THE FAMILY TRADITION

# CONTENTS

# FOREWORD

By JOHN WINTHROP ALDRICH

Much of my childhood and youth was spent at Rokeby, my family's ancestral home and farm overlooking the Hudson River and one of the Livingston family country seats highlighted in this beautiful and history-filled book. My devotion and that of my brother and sister to "the place"—to use our parlance, as everything outside our boundaries was somewhere else and indisputably of lesser consequence—came early and has remained intense for seventy years.

Cherishing and perpetuating Rokeby has been something of a genetic imperative, passed along to us by our redoubtable grandmother, Margaret Livingston Chanler Aldrich, whose stewardship lasted from 1875 until 1963. Now protected by a conservation easement and held by a family partnership whose younger members represent the eleventh generation of family land ownership that commenced with a Royal Patent in 1688, Rokeby was and is a joyous place where youngsters play, explore, exercise their imaginations, and absorb the sense of freedom and the genius loci of their heritage. It was thus for the ten Chanler orphans in the 1870s and 1880s, then successively in my father's time and our own and our children's, and it is thus today, enriching the lives of our grandchildren.

The main house, now entering its third century of existence, is capacious and idiosyncratic enough in its layout, and sufficiently crowded with many thousands of books and accumulated artifacts from the past to satisfy any young explorer. Out of doors, the charms of the old farm buildings (the center of an active dairy farm until 1961, and now in part home to a niece's thriving puppet workshop), the designed woodland paths, and remnant gardens (today supplemented by another niece's vibrant market garden), bring the past into the lively present. The Mudder Kill with its stone bridges, "Devil's Gorge," pond, dam, and waterfall, and the delights of Astor Point lying beyond the bridge crossing the railroad tracks, with its river beach, bluff-top picnic and camping spot, and old pier used for sailing jaunts, summer and winter, all held and still hold irresistible allure.

My own recollections form a collage: climbing in the immense and embracing ginkgo tree on the south lawn, romping with retrievers and terriers, summertime sails in my father's aging sloop *Iolanthe* and in his iceboats on the frozen Hudson, tree house and clubhouse projects, adventures with old carriages harnessed to a farm horse, and helping to bring in topsy-turvy wagonloads of baled hay. I remember evening games of "dumb crambo," being read to from Cooper, Scott, and Dickens, and when older, taking turns in reading parts in Shakespeare's plays, and hearing music, played on the pianos in the drawing room, that drifted upstairs to bedrooms suffused in light from the glorious sunsets over the Catskills to the west. And always and everywhere were the stories from the past recounting events and personalities that make up the lore of the family associated with Rokeby across the generations—the eccentrics, the famous, the imagined presences, the sadnesses, and the comedies.

It was and is an extended family, the details of which are well documented and kept alive in memory. Intermarriage within the Livingston clan during the past three centuries seems to have been encouraged in order to retain control of land; as it happens, my parents between them directly descended from three of the four sons of Robert, First Lord of Livingston Manor (the fourth son was childless), and from his nephew. Little wonder that we have had unusual relatives. Surely it is this family solidarity and passionate love of native place that has resulted in the establishment of so many houses by descendants of the emigrant Livingston within the twenty-five-mile neighborhood encompassed by this book. Edmund Burke in his *Reflections on the Revolution in France*, referring to the English landed gentry, might well have been writing of the Livingstons: "The power of perpetuating our property in our families is one of the most valuable and interesting circumstances belonging to it."

---

**PAGE 2** The library at Rokeby was the favorite retreat of William Backhouse Astor, Sr. The marble sculpture of the head of Hermes on the desk was once the centerpiece of Elizabeth and John Jay Chapman's library at Sylvania. **PAGES 4–5** The view of the Hudson River and the Catskill Mountains from the gardens of Holcroft. **PAGE 6** The entrance portico at Forth House is supported by Ionic columns. **OPPOSITE** The commanding view from the fifth floor of Rokeby's tower looks onto the property's lawn, with the Hudson River and the Catskill Mountains in the distance.

Sylvania was built for Elizabeth and John Jay Chapman by architect Charles A. Platt in 1905. The Chapmans purchased the adjacent property, Edgewater, in 1902 and lived there while designing their new home situated on an elevated position overlooking the Hudson River.

It is a source of deep satisfaction to me that the house and grounds at Rokeby today are in substantially better condition than they were fifty years ago, thanks to the continuous effort and talent on the part of many. Pieter Estersohn's photographs ably testify to the appearance of these refurbished rooms and views.

Indeed, a significant benefit to be derived from the publication of this book is the fostering of preservation and, where needed, careful restoration of the best of our built heritage and landscape in this region, and throughout the United States. It is no coincidence that many of the houses documented here are major components of the Hudson River National Historic Landmark District, one of the nation's largest and most diverse areas so designated (in 1990) by the secretary of the interior, and that local governments have adapted their planning and zoning policies to reflect the importance to the communities' quality of life in advancing protection for these landmark resources.

As an adult, in 1973, architect and preservation activist Richard Crowley and I incorporated Hudson River Heritage, a local group dedicated to preservation, land conservation, architectural documentation, and related education. In time not only did this lead to the successful creation of the National Historic Landmark District and the engagement of the local towns in advancing our objectives; it also led me and others to work hard on initiatives to support four specific properties documented in this book. The initiatives were to establish the Friends of Clermont, on the board of which I long served and of which my wife was the president for several terms; to preserve and restore Wilderstein, which has become an outstanding success (I was Wilderstein Preservation's founding president

and am a devoted cousin of its benefactress, Margaret Suckley); to advocate with unabated vigor over the years for the restoration and reuse of The Point, the former Hoyt family property designed by Calvert Vaux; and, since 1970, to work with three successive owners to ensure the protection and public enjoyment of Montgomery Place, the finest Romantic-era country seat in existence. The future well-being of these four landmarks, like that of so many other noteworthy buildings at risk in our country, has depended upon the unrelenting efforts and goodwill of many.

Of course, our young lives were not entirely circumscribed by Rokeby's boundaries. Among the places we knew best were the immediate adjoining properties—Sylvania to the north and Steen Valetje to the south. Sylvania was the 260-acre property purchased in 1902 by my grandmother's sister Elizabeth Chanler and her husband, the political reformer, moralist, and writer John Jay Chapman. Edgewater had been the principal structure on the premises, but after the advent of the railroad in 1851 it had become less appealing as a residence, and by 1905, Sylvania, a splendid Classical Revival house designed by Charles A. Platt, arose on the high ground, set within Platt's brilliant landscape plan. Edgewater became a secondary house, available for use by friends. The new house was embellished by a beautiful small reception room painted floor to ceiling with tropical flora, fish, and birds by Elizabeth's artist brother, Robert Chanler. A private road connected Rokeby with the Barrytown Post Office and railroad station, passing through Sylvania's lands. From the 1930s until his death in 1982, Sylvania and its dairy farm were the property of Elizabeth's colorful son,

Steen Valetje was built on land gifted to Laura Astor Delano by her father
William Backhouse Astor, Sr., upon her marriage to Franklin Hughes Delano.
The name of the property, which references the early
Dutch name of the area, translates to "little stony glen" in English.

Chanler Armstrong Chapman, publisher of the local monthly *Barrytown Explorer* and model for the eccentric millionaire title character in Saul Bellow's comic novel *Henderson the Rain King*. (For several years Bellow had rented an apartment from Chapman; theirs was a contentious relationship.)

The main house at Steen Valetje, located at the center of the estate's 550 acres, could not have provided greater contrast to Sylvania. (The house takes its name from a feature marking the property's original south boundary, and is Dutch for "little stony glen.") The earliest part of the house, designed by Frank Wills, was finished in 1851 on Rokeby land given to Franklin and Laura Astor Delano by her father William Backhouse Astor, Sr. By the 1880s it had grown into an outsized brick Tuscan-style villa, painted the color of mustard, with towers, iron balconies, working shutters, verandas, and a remarkable cast-iron and glass awning over the formal entrance stairs. The interior, much of it following the design of John H. Sturgis, was a colorful exercise in Minton tile floors, neo-Pompeian painted ceilings, carved wood and marble mantels and trim, and walls hung with gilt-framed Italian paintings. The property descended to Franklin Delano's nephew Warren, and then to Warren's son Lyman and in our childhood to the latter's widow, Leila, a great favorite of ours. Her grandchildren were our contemporaries and friends who would visit Steen Valetje. Neither they nor we were allowed to enter the long-closed "South Parlor" (the ballroom), and in ascending the grand staircase we had to avoid stepping on the center carpet. The Delano family never changed a thing in the appearance and operation of the house and grounds, with the exception of replacing homemade gas

illumination with electricity in the late 1940s. After Mrs. Delano's death in 1966, the house passed out of the family, when it was radically and regrettably transformed, and is now known as Atalanta. The northern portion of the property today comprises Poets' Walk Park.

I close this foreword to a wonderfully informative and evocative book with an excerpt from a January 1876 letter written by my great-grandfather, former Congressman John Winthrop Chanler, to one of his newly motherless sons, age twelve and lonesome at boarding school. Describing a walk in the snow, it expresses eloquently the emotional and almost mystical connections to place, to the lares and penates—the household gods of yore—that have held the Livingstons in thrall across the generations: "The mountains & River looked very beautiful, as the clouds & sunshine mingled and broke away. Sometimes it was all dark & misty; then checkered with light & shadow. The mountains that rise up in the west towards Delaware County were some of them very white with the new fallen snow, some purple, some grey, some deep blue, scattered along the horizon as far back as we could see. The tops of the Catskill range were hidden in clouds most of the day, and made the foreground of the River view look very bleak. Today is very bright & cold. Everything looks so still & cool! I have seen only two or three crows, & one little squirrel played about in the snow . . ."

We hope that the future will be a happy and secure one for the historic and distinctive places that this book documents so well, delighting both today's enthusiasts and our posterity. For Rokeby, this is assuredly my family's profoundest wish and expectation.

# INTRODUCTION

By PIETER ESTERSOHN

WHEN MY SON, ELIO, WAS YOUNG, we would walk to school out the back door of our Gramercy Park home, exiting on Nineteenth Street past many houses designed by architect Frederick Sterner during the early twentieth century. A curious pair of demilune bas-reliefs over the doors of a double townhouse at 147–149 East Nineteenth Street caught Elio's eye; he was particularly fascinated by the depiction of giraffes. This building, once known as The House of Fantasy, was owned by Robert Chanler, who had grown up at Rokeby, and his good friend Charles Cary Rumsey sculpted the bas-reliefs. At the turn of the twentieth century, the house contained a menagerie and was the site of a bohemian consortium that included Charlie Chaplin, Theda Bara, painter George Bellows, Ethel Barrymore, and Gertrude Vanderbilt Whitney.

Many connected threads have since surfaced that are Proustian in their magnitude. Certainly my Manhattan neighborhood is filled with addresses that only began to make sense once I immersed myself in the lives of Livingston family members, their genealogy, and the architects and designers they commissioned to design their country seats, the proper nineteenth-century term for these country estates. Prophetically, the ceramic beavers I grew up noticing that decorate the Astor Place subway station pay homage to the Astors' early vocation, along with that of the Livingstons, who inhabited nearby Lafayette Place, Broadway, and Bond Street in the mid-nineteenth century. Little did I know that many of my favorite writers, including Henry James, Edith Wharton, and Gore Vidal, as well as artists such as Frederic Edwin Church, Thomas Cole, and Brice Marden, have been lured by the magical embrace of the Hudson River Valley.

During my search for a weekend home, which entailed visiting well over 100 houses from Annapolis to Troy, I found Staats Hall in 2010. It happened to be built in 1839, the year photography was invented, and is located on a road with my father's name, which finally convinced me to become an owner of an historic house, with its inevitable challenges. Staats Hall was built in the Doric style on land purchased from Robert L. Livingston in 1831.

Robert was married to Margaret Maria Livingston Livingston. I thought nothing of the repetitive nature of Mrs. Livingston's last name at the time, but now laugh at the redundancy that runs throughout the genealogy of this family. Henry Staats, who had built the house with proceeds from his successful agricultural business in Red Hook, descended from Barent Staats, who had purchased one-quarter of Pieter Schuyler's Royal Patent in 1725 in this area.

In 2014, I was asked to join the Friends of Clermont, a supporting branch of Clermont State Historic Site, the earliest existing Livingston country seat. As I steeped myself in Livingston family lore, the genesis of this project was ignited. Turning to the Livingston family genealogy, a hefty 300-page volume first published in 1982, I discovered that there are sixty-three Robert Livingston entries alone. Throughout my book, I have tried to explain the complex Livingston family relationships that inform the stories behind the photographs on these pages, a tall order as even the most seasoned genealogists have difficulties identifying which Robert, Gilbert, Henry, Philip, or Margaret is related to which other family member. Due to the obscurity of many of these homes, my goal was to find the right balance between the photography, extensive historic research, and contemporary anecdotes from the present homeowners.

In previous centuries, the Hudson River provided the principal artery north for the emerging traveling class. Popular maps identified homes of importance that lined the river's coast. Now the view from the train along the Hudson is considered by many to be the most beautiful in the country. The S. S. Columbia Project was recently established to finance the refurbishment of the 115-year-old steamship and reintroduce the grand tradition of excursions on the Hudson River, much as one might have made in the nineteenth century. For those inclined to take advantage of the publicly accessible Poets' Walk, the breathtaking views of the Catskills, which the Livingstons referred to as "our mountains," are readily available to all.

Coincidentally, when my family was recently in Washington, D.C., we visited the Hirshhorn Museum and Sculpture Garden on the National Mall. Projected on several immense screens were video tableaux from the installation *The Visitors* by artist Ragnar Kjartansson, which had been filmed at Rokeby. The experience of viewing this installation spoke to me of the stewardship, commitment, and most importantly, the adaptability necessary to maintain the homes featured in this book. Although illustrating a wide range of conditions, from the vulnerability of The Point to the perfectly restored architecture of Chiddingstone, these homes share a lineage and offer an important chapter in the evolution of American architecture as well as interior and landscape design.

Livingston descendant Julia Delafield observed in 1877, in words that resonate today, "There was not one of them who did not think, and sometimes say, that his or her country seat was the choicest spot of the Hudson River, and if there was nothing like it on the Hudson River, then there was nothing like it in the world, for there was no river to compare with the Hudson."

**OPPOSITE** Staats Hall was built in 1839 by Henry Staats on land purchased from Robert L. Livingston. **LEFT** Visitors are greeted by a bison mount from 1900, which dominates the entrance hall. An 1830 French Empire bronze chandelier illuminates *Boat Race at Beach Point* by Betty Estersohn, dated 1958, on the opposite wall. **ABOVE** The portrait of Elio and Pieter Estersohn, painted by Mark Beard in 2008, hangs in the dining room.

# A BRIEF HISTORY

The Livingston family can be traced back to Scotland and the twelfth-century Saxon nobleman Leving, whose manor was known as Leving's-tun. By the thirteenth century, surnames came into use and his descendants identified themselves as "de Levingstoun." The family was granted the Barony of Callendar in 1458, and the Earldoms of Linlithgow in 1600, Callendar in 1641, and Teviot in 1696—names that were eventually transferred to Livingston country seats and townships in America. The family crest (featured on this book's casewrap) depicts a demi-savage with a laurel-wreathed head and torso—in his right hand, a club, and in his left hand, a serpent.

Robert Livingston, the founder of the American branch of the family, was born in 1654 at Ancrum, on the Teviot River in Scotland. Robert accompanied his parents to Rotterdam, Holland, in 1661 when his father, Reverend John Livingston, was exiled for opposing the Stuart Restoration's religious beliefs. In Rotterdam Robert became bilingual, learning Dutch while he apprenticed at several businesses.

Arriving in Massachusetts in 1673, Robert traveled to Albany, then the capitol of the Province of New York. He held the positions of secretary to the Van Rensselaers, wealthy Dutch landowners, and secretary of Indian Affairs, a post affording him trading opportunities.

In 1679, Robert married Alida Schuyler Van Rensselaer, sister of Pieter Schuyler, soon to be the mayor of Albany. She was the widow of Nicholas Van Rensselaer, providing Robert an allegiance with the two most prominent families in the region. Recognizing that power in the Colonies lay with land acquisition, he negotiated with the Mahicans for the purchase of many acres in 1683. Robert then petitioned Governor Dongen and received in 1686 a Royal Patent that included 2,000 acres at the confluence of the North River, later called the Hudson River, and the Roeliff Jansen Kill, as well as an unconnected 600-acre tract near the Massachusetts border, and mysteriously all the land in between. Whether this was through an oversight or nefarious intention has been the subject of much conjecture, but the end result was a swath of land that encompassed 162,248 acres. This untamed land became a future source of great wealth for the Livingston family as dominant landholders.

The Manor of Livingston was established as the fourth land grant to be created in the Province of New York. The designation of "manor" gave the landowner semi-feudal authority and judicial powers over his territory. Simultaneously, Jacob and Hendryk Kip negotiated with the Esopus people in 1686 for lands in what is presently Rhinebeck, and in 1703, Henry Beekman, Margaret Beekman Livingston's grandfather, was granted a Royal Patent for 20,000 acres in the same town.

The first time Robert sailed for England to attend to business in 1694, he met with a disastrous shipwreck, which prompted him to change his family's motto from *Si Je Puis* (If I can) to *Spero Meliora* (I hope for better things). In 1699, he built a home, referred to as the Livingston Manor house, on his Hudson River property. The house, constructed of stone with a long central hall decorated with antlers and bearskins, is where Robert, First Lord of Livingston Manor conducted his business affairs. Abandoned, it was taken down in 1800.

Robert's strategy for land acquisition continued in the eighteenth century in the Hudson Valley and concluded in 1715 when he sailed to England to reconfirm his property ownership with King George I. The division of Livingston land began when Robert "of Clermont," a younger son of the First Lord, was gifted 13,000 acres on the death of his father in 1728, where he built his home, Clermont. In 1786, primogeniture was abolished in New York State, changing the way Livingston property was passed on to future generations. Subsequently, Margaret Beekman Livingston divided the 240,000 acres she had inherited from her father among her ten children. In 1843, Edward P. Livingston's five children followed suit when they subdivided his property north of Clermont. In 1846, a constitutional amendment made land leases on farmland illegal, giving incentive for the family to further subdivide its properties.

Today, there are more than one million Livingston descendants living in America who can trace their roots back to Robert. I have thrown a proverbial net into the sea of research on the Livingstons' legacy, and continue to collect its bounty. I tip my hat to future discoveries.

---

The bird's-eye view at the confluence of the Roeliff Jansen Kill and the Hudson River takes in the riverfront site in the distance of the original Livingston Manor house, built by Robert Livingston, First Lord of Livingston Manor, and his wife, Alida Schuyler Van Rensselaer Livingston.

# CLERMONT
## 1730

THE HISTORY OF THE LIVINGSTONS at Clermont begins with the sighting of a pair of moccasins descending from a chimney of the Livingston Manor house, located at the confluence of the Hudson River and the Roeliff Jansen Kill. Julia Delafield, a Livingston descendant and family biographer, recounts this tale in her 1877 *Biographies of Francis Lewis and Morgan Lewis*: "The first summer that young Robert [Livingston] passed with his father at the Manor [after his return from Scotland], his attention was attracted one afternoon by what seemed to him an unusual number of Indians skulking around and keeping within the shadow of the woods. That night, after he was in bed, he heard a noise in the chimney. He lay quite still and watched; presently a pair of legs descended upon the hearth. Robert sprang from his bed, seized the fellow before he could extricate himself, exclaiming at the same time 'Villain, confess!' . . . Robert's father was so pleased with his son's intrepidity that he gave him the lower end of the manor—a tract consisting of about thirteen thousand acres." This gift contained an entail that, from 1728 until the end of the Revolution, would dictate that the property pass directly down through the line of male descendants of Robert Livingston, Jr. The only legal option to provide income for the inheritors of the property were leaseholds with tenant farmers, as the land could not be subdivided.

Robert "of Clermont," as he became known, took possession of the land in 1728 when his father, Robert, First Lord of Livingston Manor, died. In 1730, he made improvements on a late Dutch stone house on the property and moved in. His initial thought was to name the house Callendar, after an ancestral property in Scotland, but this was labeled pretentious by his elder brother Philip, the Second Lord. After an additional attempt at naming the house Ancram, after another family property in Scotland, he settled on the name Claremont, which eventually was changed to Clermont. In 1750, he made further improvements to the house by refining the details, rendering it a proper Georgian home. Over the years, Clermont has been erroneously referred to as the Southern Manor due to its location several miles south of the actual manor house.

Clermont was continuously inhabited by seven direct generations of Livingstons from 1730 until 1942, when the last generation moved into cottages on the property. It is unique that the collection of the family's personal effects and travel memorabilia encompassing this entire period is intact, and was passed on to the State of New York in 1962.

Robert, known as "The Judge," was the only child born to Robert of Clermont. In 1759, he had been promoted to the position of judge of the Admiralty Court, and in 1763 he became judge of the Supreme Court of the Province of New York. The following year, he appealed to the king asking for certain rights for the colonists. His wife, and second cousin, was the formidable Margaret Beekman. Their affectionate relationship was best expressed by his words to her, "You are the cordial drop with which Heaven has graciously thought fit to sweeten my cup." Further sweetening the alliance was the fact that she had brought with her a hefty dowry and the promise of the addition of thousands of acres to the Livingston holdings.

The winter of 1775–76 was chaotic for Margaret. The deaths of her husband, father, and son-in-law, General Robert Montgomery, had her racing between three country seats. The death of her spouse allowed her to be the rare woman who inherited on her own as a widow; normally the inheritance would have gone to her husband and bypassed her. It was thus established that Margaret was an unusual woman who held the purse strings during this period. Over time the couple had amassed 753,000 acres through inheritance and acquisition across the Hudson River and the Catskill Mountains.

---

**PREVIOUS SPREAD** The west elevation features two recumbent lions, purchased by John Henry Livingston in Italy in the 1920s, that guard the original Hudson River entrance. **ABOVE** The engraving of a Clermont ram is from Robert "The Chancellor" Livingston's copy of his 1809 volume on animal husbandry. **OPPOSITE** A portrait of Robert Livingston, First Lord of Livingston Manor (left), hangs in the entrance hall across from a portrait of Philip, the Second Lord.

The magnificent view from Clermont encompassed most of the 1708 Hardenbergh Patent, two-million acres granted by Queen Anne across the river. Robert of Clermont had accumulated more than 500,000 acres, about one-third of this patent, in 1740, creating a vista that the family referred to as "our mountains."

Edward Livingston, a grandson of The Judge, described Robert in Thomas Streatfeild Clarkson's *A Biographical History of Clermont, or Livingston Manor* as follows: "He marked the epoch at which he retired from the world, by preserving its costume—the flowing, well powdered wig . . . cut-velvet waistcoat . . . breeches barely covering the knee, silk stockings, and shining square-toed shoes."

Margaret referred to the home as Claremount before the Revolution and Clermont after, which is reflective of the fluidity in naming properties during the period. When General John Vaughan advanced the British up the Hudson River in 1777, he arrived at Clermont after devastating Kingston with fire. Fortunately, because of a warning sent north from The Pynes, Margaret had just enough time to escape after hiding the silver and paintings down what presumably was a dry well.

Upon her return she was met with utter ruin—several of the exterior walls were all that remained of her home. A testament to her sturdy constitution, she quickly built a hut with full intentions of living there. Margaret represents the bridge that separates two distinct periods of Colonial life. The previous generations spent time and energy dealing with survival while her offspring were focused on becoming cultivated by learning French, music, and philosophy. Soon, confident of her sense of entitlement as she had proposed that General George Clinton be nominated as governor at a meeting at Clermont, she asked him to excuse her workers from the military in order to immediately reconstruct her Georgian house in 1778. Indebted, he felt somewhat obliged to send back the masons, plasterers, carpenters, and brick burners to assist her in rebuilding.

When George and Martha Washington stayed at Clermont in 1782, Margaret wrote to her son Robert that "Washington admired the place and Mrs. Washington seemed pleased." Seemingly this cemented her social dominance over the manor branch of the family, who resided farther up the Hudson River. Margaret's famous Clermont muffins were served to the Washingtons. They were "not pastry, nor like the Scottish short-bread, nor the beaten biscuit of the South . . . cut out with the top of a wine glass and nothing but silver and glass must touch them in the making."

As a woman in an unusual position to make executive decisions, Margaret gifted property to her ten children. Janet built Grasmere, Margaret built Linwood, Henry Beekman was left the Kip-Beekman-Livingston house in Rhinecliff, Catherine built Wildercliff, Gertrude was responsible for Staatsburgh, Alida built Rokeby, and Edward eventually inhabited Montgomery Place. Margaret died content one evening in 1800, with twenty-four descendants living nearby in vast and luxurious homes. Sitting at the head of her table in the dining room, she fell backward and expired.

---

The study has a collection of 500 books from Robert "The Chancellor" Livingston's collection. The cabinet in the center of the room holds sculptures by Alice Delafield Livingston. The sewing table was a wedding present to Cornelia Livingston. On top of the right bookcase is a terra-cotta sculpture of Honoria by her mother, Alice.

The eldest son of The Judge and Margaret Beekman Livingston was named Robert and became known as "The Chancellor." He was perhaps the most illustrious family member. "He was sufficiently contented with his ancestral position," wrote George Dangerfield in his biography *Chancellor Robert R. Livingston of New York, 1746–1813.* As chancellor, or leading judicial official of New York, Robert Robert Livingston administered the oath of office to George Washington in 1789, not far from The Chancellor's Manhattan home at 3 Broadway. Robert held this elected post for twenty-four years, following his membership in the Second Continental Congress. He also held membership in the Committee of Five, which drafted the Declaration of Independence although he did not write a word of the document and was unable to sign it, having been called back to New York as chancellor.

In 1781, The Chancellor was appointed the country's first minister of foreign affairs, a post that evolved into that of secretary of state. Although a slave owner, Livingston had penned an early, unsuccessful bill in 1785 that was to gradually abolish slavery. The same year, he organized the Manumission Society of New York. In 1801, he was asked by Thomas Jefferson to accept the position of minister plenipotentiary to France, where he spent five years mingling with the court of Napoleon. The Chancellor became friends with the First Consul Napoleon and his brothers Louis and Joseph, who later, in exile, spent many months as guests at Clermont. He

---

**ABOVE** A late eighteenth-century French mantel clock, attributed to Gavelle L'Aîné, was made to commemorate the 1783 flight of the hot-air balloon *La Charlière.* **RIGHT** The early nineteenth-century Baccarat chandelier in the drawing room was purchased by Edward Philip Livingston. A portrait of Philip Livingston, a signer of the Declaration of Independence, hangs near an overdoor that was copied in 1893 from those at Oak Hill.

was not intimidated at court—he could not imagine that any man was a finer social specimen than himself.

It is during his residence in Paris that The Chancellor, along with James Monroe, oversaw the negotiations with Talleyrand and Marbois leading to the Louisiana Purchase, which was to double the size of the United States. Robert's role in the negotiation was shrouded in conjecture, since he had misrepresented the date of the agreement, taking undue credit at the expense of Monroe.

While in France, Chancellor Livingston developed a friendship with Robert Fulton with whom he financed, and collaborated on the design of the first steamboat, named the *North River*, and eventually renamed the *Clermont*. Their first partially successful experiments were held on the Seine in June 1800. Fulton stayed with Livingston at Clermont in 1807 and refurbished the steamboat at the dock at Red Hook Landing, now Tivoli. Fulton's biographer Alice Crary Sutcliffe described the onlookers on the day the ship docked at Clermont, noting that some "prostrated themselves and besought Providence to protect them from the approach of the horrible monster, which was marching on the tide and lighting its path by the fire that it vomited." There is a more bucolic version of this scene in a 1939 mural painted by Olin Dows at the Rhinebeck Post Office—part of President Franklin Delano Roosevelt's WPA program.

When he returned to America, Chancellor Livingston assumed, at Clermont, the persona of a gentleman farmer of the Enlightenment with an endless curiosity about the mysteries of the physical world. He became the president of the New York Society for the Promotion of Agriculture, was elected a member of the Society of the Cincinnati in 1784, and was a founder of the American Academy of Fine Arts in 1808 and the Manhattan Company (a precursor of the Chase Manhattan Bank) in 1799. He was exceptionally proud of the fields of clover that he had developed to feed his prize flock of Merino sheep. Napoleon had presented him with the gift of two rams and two ewes after The Chancellor visited the emperor's flock at Rambouillet. Livingston also imported sheep from the em-

**LEFT** The south wing of the house was added in 1831 as apartments, then converted to a billiards room, before becoming the family's living room at the end of the nineteenth century. **ABOVE** In the same room is a red Morocco frame containing family photographs taken in Europe in the 1920s.

press's flock at the Château de Malmaison. Along with the triumphs, there were several failures, including an unsuccessful attempt with neighbor Pierre Delabigarre at paper production using conserva, better known then as frog's spit. George Dangerfield observed in his biography *Chancellor Robert R. Livingston of New York* that The Chancellor's "imagination was that of the eighteenth-century amateur scientist who believed that the physical universe might at any moment yield one of its innumerable gifts, extraordinary secrets from some fortuitous experiment or sudden flash of insight."

When The Chancellor died in 1813, his estate was left to his two daughters. Elizabeth "Betsy" and Margaret Maria married their Livingston cousins, maintaining the family name without need of a male heir. Elizabeth and her husband, Edward Philip, inherited Clermont. Their marriage healed a rift between the two branches of the family that had originated over mill rights at the Roeliff Jansen Kill, which separated the two properties. Elizabeth predeceased her husband, whose second wife was Mary Crook Broome. Edward's will stated that upon his death Mary was to inherit Clermont, but this was vehemently contested by Elizabeth's children. After prolonged legal machinations, Mary eventually agreed to accept 20,000 dollars to extricate herself physically, legally, and emotionally from Clermont, leaving the surrounding area to be subdivided among the five surviving children of Elizabeth and Edward. This subdivision yielded the eventual construction of Ridgely, Chiddingstone, Southwood, Midwood, Holcroft, Oak Terrace, and Northwood.

The final chapter of the nineteenth-century Anti-Rent Wars concluded during this subdivision, forcing the hand of the Livingstons in selling off acreage to tenant farmers who had previously maintained them under the feudal system dating back to the seventeenth

century. The Calico Indians, as this group of Anti-Renters were known, led by Chief Big Thunder, finally became landowners, thus ending the tight fist the Livingstons had held over their vast holdings.

In 1783 The Chancellor built New Clermont near the site of Belvedere, his previous house that had been burned by the British in 1777. His youngest daughter, Margaret Maria, inherited New Clermont upon her father's death in 1813, after marrying Robert Livingston Livingston, who had grown up at Teviotdale.

In naming his house New Clermont (later called Clermont, Idele, Idyle, and finally Arryl House), The Chancellor intended to distinguish his home from that of his mother. The name Clermont hints at the French spellings for the words "clear" and "mountain." The Chancellor was responsible for building the house, which was conceptually very French in design. He collaborated on the plan with engineer Marc Isambard Brunel, who had worked with him on an early version of the steamship and had designed Massena in Barrytown for his brother John.

New Clermont was sited just south of the footprint of Belvedere. It was formed in the shape of the letter "H" and had one of the finest private libraries in the country with over 6,000 volumes. The terraces that connected the projecting wings were planted with lemon, orange, and myrtle trees in tubs, and there was a gigantic greenhouse on the south elevation. In his biography *The Livingstons of Livingston Manor*, Edwin Brockholst Livingston remarked that the dining room tables were "set on great occasions . . . so constructed that large plants rose from their centers." William Strickland, a visitor in 1794, described New Clermont as "being hung with French papers . . . Dinner was at three and supper at nine served by four boys, four to twelve years old, barefoot in October but in green livery with red details." There was a fine balance at New Clermont that blended formality and simplicity. Dangerfield noted that here Livingston accomplished this with a "Byronic detachment."

Following The Chancellor's death, A. J. (Andrew Jackson) Downing, horticulturist extraordinaire of the period, described Clermont as having a "level or gently undulating lawn, four or five miles in length . . . the long vistas of planted avenues, added to its fine water view, rendered this a noble place . . . The finest yellow locusts in America are now standing in the pleasure-grounds here . . . "

To celebrate the visit of the Marquis de Lafayette, a fancy dress ball was held in his honor at New Clermont in 1824. His sister Janet Montgomery ended the evening by dancing with the guest of honor before being transported back home in The Chancellor's gilded coach drawn by four white horses. John Henry Livingston surmised that "although politically the strictest of Democrats, the style of living congenial to him continued to be that of the Lords of the manor."

The paradox of The Chancellor's life back home was that he was forward-looking in his scientific explorations while intrinsically tied to the past as a landowner with firm roots in a feudal structure of society and property. When Belvedere was burned by the British, The Chancellor made his way to the town of Staatsburgh and the

LEFT One of eleven bathrooms installed during the late nineteenth century. OPPOSITE The skylighted kitchen was originally added by Edward Philip Livingston as Clermont's estate office in the early nineteenth century, and was converted into a kitchen in the 1890s.

parson's house, where he took stock of his melancholy situation. At this point he offered Belvedere on 105 acres to his friend John Alsop in order to start to gather funds, as he was cash poor, but Alsop did not accept the offer. Starting in 1779, the landed were being assessed taxes for the first time, and Margaret Beekman wrote in a letter "Cozen [*sic*] Robert is to be taxed 16,000 pounds sterling," a challenge on a salary of 4,000 dollars a year as secretary of state in 1781.

Margaret Maria's son Eugene Augustus had initially inherited New Clermont but traded with his brother Montgomery for his land to the south, where he built Eversleigh, later Teviot. Montgomery was a fine artist who had spent the 1830s studying painting in Europe. He established a "delightful painting room" and decorated many interior doors at New Clermont with landscape scenes. He had let New Clermont fall into disrepair before Emily and Anna Clarkson purchased it at auction in 1857, two years after he died. They named the house Idele after putting it back in perfect repair.

Clermont, the eldest son of Elizabeth and Edward, inherited his family's home Clermont in 1843 with his wife Cornelia Livingston, who had grown up in nearby Oak Hill. To further complicate the genealogical spider's web, upon Cornelia's death, Clermont married his cousin Montgomery's widow, Mary Colden Swarthout, who left New Clermont in 1851 to move into "old" Clermont. His third wife, Anna Clarkson, owner of what was now called Idele, induced him to move back into her home. When Clermont died in 1895, Idele was put up for sale with 207 acres, but was not sold.

John Henry, the only son of Clermont and Cornelia Livingston, was joined at Clermont by his third wife, Alice Delafield Clarkson Livingston, following their marriage in 1906. At six feet tall and in possession of a name that settled any question of dominance in the region, she reigned under the locally agreed-upon title "Lady Alice." Alice deftly maneuvered Katherine Livingston Timpson, John Henry's daughter from a previous marriage, out of the picture so that her children would be in line to inherit Clermont. Alice's cousin Robert Reginald Livingston, a neighbor up Woods Road at Northwood, was known to volunteer, "I'll never forget that lovely, sunny summer day when cousin Alice married cousin John," to illustrate the climate of extended family that had been carved into the psyche of the inhabitants along the river. Alice was an avid gardener, adding four formal exterior spaces to the property including an Italian-walled garden, a wilderness garden, and a cutting garden. The couple purchased Idele in 1908, therefore uniting components of the estate. They renamed the property Arryl House, a loose acronym for Robert Robert Livingston. The unoccupied house burned 1909, but the ruins are still visible and have recently been structurally reinforced.

John Henry Livingston was responsible for adding the second- and third-floor additions to the south wing bringing the total number of rooms to forty-four. An enormous veranda had been added in 1893 to the west side of the house. In 1920, by bringing coals to Newcastle a Colonial Revival cosmetic renovation was initiated, further obscuring the original Georgian character of the structure. Conrad Hanson, former executive director of the Friends of Clermont, discovered in 2012 the signature of architect Mott B. Schmidt on unrealized designs he made for John Henry while working on the Obolensky's home, Marienruh. Schmidt, a Georgian purist, proposed changing the west elevation of Clermont to a composition more in line with the house's appearance in 1831.

Two daughters, Honoria, born in 1909, and Janet, born a year later, were the last Livingston inhabitants of Clermont. Between their mother and father's lineages, they were seven-times Livingstons. Due to financial constraints the family moved to Fiesole, outside of Florence, in 1912 so that they could live economically on a scale to which they were accustomed, returning to Clermont in 1921. Following the Great Depression, due to increasing maintenance costs, the main house was closed in 1942, and subsequently, the family was relegated to the property's Sylvan Cottage and the Gardener's Cottage.

Honoria's regal speech patterns and presentation were emphasized by a spectacularly long and elegant neck worthy of the attention of painters such as Sargent and Boldini. She wore a peach basket atop her head when the walnut trees started producing their ripe bounty. Eventually, Frances "Fuzz" Davis, from neighboring Teviot, offered her a bright yellow hard hat on which he had "McV," a reference to her married name, painted on the back. She lived at Sylvan Cottage, located on the entrance driveway to Clermont, with her husband, Reginald "Rex" McVitty. Honoria was six feet, one inch tall and Rex was six feet, four inches tall, so

it was with much caution that they inhabited the cottage, with its very low ceilings. Rex was a mycologist (mushroom specialist) with a wonderful Irish brogue, whose expert opinion was often consulted upon discovery of a suspicious mushroom by a family member. Bright blue forget-me-nots filled the low stone walls to the south of the cottage and the porch was a bower of potted flowers. Rex had been disinvited from further visits to Vincent Astor's yacht, the *Nourmahal*, which Astor kept anchored at his home Ferncliff when it had been discovered that he had driven away in his black Buick convertible with two cold bottles of Astor's Champagne in his pockets.

Alice had changed the name of the Gardener's Cottage to Clermont Cottage when she moved there in 1942. Janet took ownership of Clermont Cottage in 1964, the year Alice died, and it is from here that she drove weekly to her job in New York City at the New York Trust Company's estate division.

Clermont Cottage is now the James D. Livingston Research Library and the office of the Friends of Clermont. Alice sold the property with 414 acres to the New York State Office of Parks, Recreation and Historic Preservation in 1962, while donating the house's collections to the state. The Clermont house is now presented to visitors as it was in the 1930s. The property was listed as a National Historic Landmark in 1973 before Honoria left an additional seventy-one acres and an endowment of two million dollars to the Friends of Clermont. She maintained Sylvan Cottage on fifteen acres of the property until she died in 2000.

---

**ABOVE** Janet and Honoria Livingston's bedroom includes a Duncan Phyfe dressing table, a gift from The Chancellor to Harriet Livingston and Robert Fulton. **OPPOSITE** Sylvan Cottage was built in 1790. It served as the family's honeymoon dwelling, and was later the house of Honoria and her husband, Reginald "Rex" McVitty.

# THE BOUWERIE

## 1762

PREVIOUS SPREAD The view of The Bouwerie from the southeast shows the house sited on a hillock, which is above a tributary to the Roeliff Jansen Kill. Brick headers placed between the windows of the second floor identify the construction date of 1762. The wing extending behind the house, which now contains the library, was built in 1705 as an earlier structure. ABOVE The Federal arches around the fireplace in the dining room were added around 1800, replacing the previous wall paneling.

IN 1694, ROBERT LIVINGSTON, in a very rare transaction he never repeated, sold close to 2,000 acres of his land in two parcels to Major Dirck Wesselse Ten Broeck, an early Dutch settler. It is unclear whether this was an act of generosity or simply the only way Livingston could secure Ten Broeck's services as the business manager of his immense estate. Ten Broeck's previous positions included serving as mayor of Beverwyck (now Albany), so named for its reputation as the province's fur-trapping capital in 1696 and commissioner of Indian Affairs. Due to his stature, Ten Broeck may not have been easily persuaded by such an offer, but in October, for a sum of fifteen pounds sterling and a nominal annual rent of ten shillings, the deal was struck.

Before the turn of the seventeenth century, the area where the Town of Clermont now lies was a vast and wild frontier. Ten Broeck was often mentioned in the frequent and intimate letters from Alida Schuyler Livingston to her husband, Robert. Among other deeds, she noted that he was responsible for "distributing provisions to 'our' Indians."

The smaller tract of land, close to 600 acres, lay southeast of where the present house, The Bouwerie, now stands, while the larger portion, 1,200 acres, was located on both sides of the stream known as the Roeliff Jansen Kill, a tributary of the Hudson River. This tract of land was somewhat far from the Hudson where the Livingston Manor house was situated, but the stream, colloquially known as Livingston's Creek, provided easy access by canoe to and from the main waterway.

Roeliff Jansen had been an assistant *bouwmeester*, or builder for the Patroon (an individual granted manorial rights under the Dutch crown) of Rensselaerwyck. During an unusually severe winter in the 1630s, Jansen's boat became frozen in the stream that was to eventually carry his name. Unable to extricate himself due to harsh weather, he was obliged to stay with the local Native Americans until the spring thaw before returning to the office of Kiliaen Van Rensselaer in Albany to report the findings of his explorations.

In 1705 Ten Broeck built a small dwelling on the *bouwerij*, or farm, from which the present house takes its name. His grandson and namesake, Dirck Wesselse Ten Broeck, inherited most of the property in 1756, buying the additional acreage from his brother and completed The Bouwerie in 1762. This building was connected, as was the custom at the time, to the older, now subordinate wing.

The approach to the house, down a long drive, past the family burial ground and icehouse, then down a treacherous escarpment (the steep hill protected the house from the north winds), delivers a transformative experience. All one can hear are the sounds of the fauna on the flats surrounding the stream and the running water winding in a serpentine manner around the house. The Dutch understood how and where to build on the lowlands.

The Bouwerie was a particularly grand house for this region at the time. It is composed of a full two stories with an attic and a gambrel roof. This was unusual; most homes during that time had only one story, with an attic for storage. In the Dutch manner each room served multiple purposes, unlike the English tradition, which assigned specific uses for each room. A new addition was constructed with bricks that are rumored to have come from Holland. A remarkable geometric design consisting of four diamonds created with glazed black brick headers graces the north elevation of the house. Above this pattern are two round porthole windows.

**ABOVE** The window valences in Edward O'Neal's bedroom are made with fragments of eighteenth-century crewel embroidery. **RIGHT** The original 1762 Dutch paneling in the bedroom is painted Prussian blue, a pigment invented in 1704.

On the front of the house, incorporated between the second-floor windows, white bricks outline the date of construction as 1762. The letters "T" and "B" indicate Ten Broeck's family name.

On March 10, 1813, The Bouwerie was sold along with 572 acres to Walter Tryon Livingston, who had grown up nearby at The Hermitage. The price pocketed by Dirck's son Samuel Ten Broeck was ten dollars, which even at the time appears to have been a paltry sum. This may explain the historical conjecture that Walter Tryon traded his house Richmond Hill for the farm. The house eventually passed to his grandson Walter Tryon Livingston Sanders, who was born in 1830, and it remained in the family until 1864 when the property was sold to the Wilson family for 27,000 dollars. On a flat plateau near what was called the King's Highway, the Ten Broecks and Livingstons indulged their chief recreation— horseracing. American Eclipse and Sir Henry were the names of two of the famous horses that ran there in the 1820s.

In 1921, Theodore Gaty purchased The Bouwerie, which had been vacant for twenty-five years. Gaty, with the help of his three

brothers, renovated the property. His daughter, Allene Gaty Hatch, was born here in 1926 and spent an idyllic childhood churning butter, collecting Balsam of Peru and buckets of maple sap, and inhaling the intoxicating smell of the hayloft. There was a swimming hole toward the south of the property with a huge tree from which to jump into the creek and nearby, Indian arrowheads littering the fields could be collected. Her father had given her the nickname "Squeaky" after observing her infant squeals, claiming later that he "had no idea the name would stick." Ninety-two years later, she is still Squeaky. She recounts numerous anecdotes in her book *Real Pearls and Darned Stockings*, a favorite being in 1931 when her uncle Clint, an avid aviator with a red biplane, returned home from the nearby airport one evening with an unexpected guest. The story still fresh in her mind, she mentions that as he walked in the front door with "the queen of the skies," Amelia Earhart, the family gasped. He announced that while choking his plane, he had learned that a violent storm was soon to arrive. Earhart had asked him if he knew of a local hotel where she could find a room to wait out the storm that had interrupted her flight. Gaty replied that the best place to stay was his brother's home nearby. Squeaky's grandmother, who wore Irish tweeds, was a theosophist, and insisted on being called "Peter," after Peter Pan. She had read that Amelia was fond of buttermilk, but the only store that might stock this was seven miles away so she decided to concoct her own version of the drink. Vinegar and several other sour ingredients were added to milk, resulting in an undrinkable disaster. There was much anticipation in how this was going to be received. "Miss Earhart took one polite sip and that was that."

Squeaky eventually married the writer Alden Hatch, who authored biographies on Lord Mountbatten, Prince Bernard of the Netherlands, Buckminster Fuller, Dwight and Mamie Eisenhower, and Marjorie Post. An eternal flirt, Squeaky offered candidly, "If I ever had a sneaker [an affair], it would be with the Prince!"

The current owner of The Bouwerie, Dianne O'Neal, purchased the house with her husband, Edward O'Neal V, in 1986 from Edyth Townsend as a weekend home when her son Edward VI was a year old. Dianne's interest in things historic led her to work at the New York Public Library examining rare manuscripts and prints.

She has since replaced a Dutch *stoep* (stoop), which was originally incorporated into the facade. The work was part of a comprehensive project taken on by O'Neal with the assistance of preservation carpenters Conrad Fingado and Emily Majer. Previous efforts at renovation have been stripped away in an effort to discover the intentions of the original builder. Dianne explained, "I was compelled to discover where the history of the house lies! Only when we peeled back the layers could we see what the original footprints were."

The library, which has had many of its details obscured over three centuries, has been painstakingly brought back to the early eighteenth century. Windows have been re-created using old glass following the original muntin profiles popular at the time. The Dutch fireplace now warms the room again, providing an historically appropriate ambience. Massive beams with their original Roman numerals have been uncovered and, through a process called dendrochronology, have been unequivocally dated to 1705, ten years after Ten Broeck purchased the property. This finding corrects previous claims that the beams were installed in 1735. The Cornell University's Tree-Ring Laboratory is working to date historic buildings and build tree ring chronologies as far back as the Late Glacial period. The process starts with a core sample of wood the size of a pencil being placed in a glass tube then compared with a data base that is made up of climatic recordings for each year. Temperature, rainfall, and insect infestation are only three of the many components recorded from inside fallen timbers.

O'Neal's renovation successfully brings the house back to the eighteenth century, now perfectly complimenting the landscape surrounding it. Sitting on the edge of the stream that winds in front of the house, the visitor is transported through all the senses to a bucolic setting from an earlier time.

---

OPPOSITE The carpentry in the library, original to the 1705 house, was skillfully restored by Emily Majer. ABOVE The north gable-end wall of the 1762 house has decorative bricks, which form graphic diamonds within the Dutch bond brickwork. The two small oval openings at the top of the wall served as lookouts. RIGHT The bricks were produced on-site in 1761 for the Ten Broeck family.

TEVIOTDALE

1774

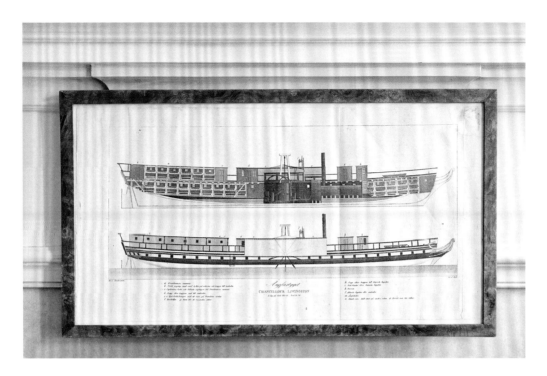

"IF IT GETS TO BE TOO MUCH, GET RID OF IT." When Richard Barker, a former owner of Teviotdale, passed away in 1988, these were among his final words to Victor Cornelius, the present owner to whom Barker willed the house. Teviotdale has fascinating historic roots, however there have been numerous practical challenges in maintaining the house over the years. When I photographed this house, Cornelius exclaimed "If you're going to give a house or any physical thing a personality, this one certainly has one!"

Teviotdale was built by Walter Livingston in 1774, a year after his father Robert Livingston, the Third (and last) Lord of Livingston Manor, sold him the land for 300 pounds sterling. The property sits between the Roeliff Jansen Kill and the Kleine Kill in the hamlet of Linlithgo about a mile and a half from the mouth of the Hudson River. It is sited on what was to become Great Lot Number One in the subdivision of the original manor in 1790. The house, constructed in the Province of New York while still under English jurisdiction, is distinctly Irish Georgian in its design, with an attention to detail linked to Great Britain's infatuation with the architecture of Andrea Palladio at the time. Walter, in fact, had studied at Cambridge University prior to his purchase of the land, leading him to become an anglophile. As time progressed, he built a piazza at the back of the house, and a balustrade on the roof. These elements contrasted strongly with the more sober and conservative designs being realized in the region. On the property Walter also built an additional thirteen dependencies, or outbuildings, which would have been appropriate for an estate of this size.

Walter married Cornelia Schuyler in 1767, and the couple lived for several years at the Livingston Manor house at the foot of the Roeliff Jansen Kill on the Hudson. During the construction of Teviotdale, he served on the Committee of One Hundred in 1775, formed with the goal of boycotting British goods. He was the first speaker of the New York Assembly, from 1777 to 1779, and member of the Continental Congress in 1784. His business interests included a sugar plantation in Jamaica and vessels that traded with India and Europe. In 1794, he ran into financial difficulties while attempting to start a new bank and lost his home until his brothers bought it back at auction in Claverack and resold it to him for one dollar.

At Teviotdale, Walter and Cornelia raised eleven children, including Henry Walter, who built The Hill, in the Town of Livingston, and Harriet, who married Robert Fulton, designer of the first commercially successful steamship. In 1808, Harriet and Robert were married in front of the fireplace in the Teviotdale drawing room. A 1790 census lists twenty-eight people living in the house on the occasion of a visit for tea from George and Martha Washington, with Martha spending the night in the yellow bedroom.

Robert Fulton had gone to London in 1787, and reinstating his acquaintance with the American painter Benjamin West, he visited West's studio armed with letters of presentation from Benjamin Franklin and Charles Peale. Despite this impressive association, Fulton floundered for a time in London until in 1791 when he met William Courtenay, Earl of Devon, who quickly became his benefactor in a manner suggesting a romantic arrangement.

Moving to Paris in the late 1790s, Fulton installed himself at Madame Hillaire's pension on the Left Bank. In Paris, he started a relationship with Ruth Barlow, his senior by a decade, who was staying at the pension as well. Ruth's husband, Joel Barlow, was considered one of America's best poets of the day and was in Algeria as a special ambassador for President Washington, with

PREVIOUS SPREAD Left: The plaster bust of Robert Fulton was cast from the original Jean-Antoine Houdon sculpture made in Paris in 1797. Right: A view of the long straight avenue leading to Teviotdale. OPPOSITE The Chinese Chippendale staircase in the entrance hall was designed by Harrison Cultra in the 1970s. ABOVE The 1812 Swedish engraving depicts Fulton's steamship *The Chancellor Livingston*. FOLLOWING SPREAD Over the library fireplace is a nineteenth-century plaster fragment with a scene of the steamboat *North River* salvaged from Troy's Union Station in 1958.

ABOVE The vase placed on a column in front of the dining room window was purchased at the estate sale held at Steen Valetje following the death of Mrs. Lyman Delano. RIGHT Robert Fulton and Harriet Livingston were married in front of this fireplace in 1807. The eighteenth-century mirrors that hung in the living and dining rooms at Teviotdale were repatriated from Lydia Redmond in 2010.

the task of negotiating the release of Americans taken prisoner by Barbary pirates. Shortly after Joel Barlow's return to Paris and subsequent introductions were made, the three of them moved out of the pension and into a nearby *hôtel particulier* on the Rue de Vaugirard, where for the following seven years they lived together in a *ménage à trois* with ". . . strong affection, that devoted attachment, that real friendship, which subsisted in a most extraordinary degree between Mr. Barlow and Mr. Fulton during their lives," as Ruth later recounted in a letter to Cadwallader Colden.

Robert Fulton had collaborated with Robert "The Chancellor" Livingston of Clermont on the *North River*, the steamboat that had set sail on August 17, 1807, from a dock on Cortlandt Street in Manhattan heading to Albany. The two men had met while living in Paris. Fulton was painting and designing torpedoes for England and Livingston was there to negotiate with Napoleon regarding the context of the Louisiana Purchase on behalf of Thomas Jefferson. Their point of introduction was punctuated by their mutual obsession with steam power, particularly when used to propel ships.

Fulton left his mark in Paris. He created two circular panoramic paintings, which were installed in large rotundas, for an exhibition in 1800. A covered walkway, the Passage des Panoramas, was built to connect Fulton's temporary installation, and the Rue Fulton was named after him. While staying in Paris, he also designed what Napoleon had called the *bâteau poisson*, or submarine. Livingston, a gentleman of the Enlightenment, had previously experimented with designs approximating a steamship but with no great success.

In 1802, Livingston and Fulton entered into a partnership agreement for a steamboat whereby Livingston would supply the financing and the monopoly for access to the Hudson River and Fulton would be in charge of the design. Both were to share in the eventual profits of the enterprise.

An often contested Livingston family legend claims that on August 18, 1807, at Clermont's dock, the *North River*, later to be named the *Clermont*, was detained for a moment of celebration while en route upriver in order for The Chancellor to announce the engagement of Walter's daughter Harriet to Robert Fulton.

The newlyweds spent time at Teviotdale with Cornelia Livingston since Walter Livingston had died in 1797. Robert filled his days painting, returning to the talent that had occupied him before becoming famous and wealthy due to his work inventing the

steamship. The first son born to the Fultons was named Robert Barlow Fulton (known as Barlow).

When Robert Fulton died in 1815 at age fifty, having contracted pneumonia after rescuing his attorney from the Hudson River, Harriet was left with four children. She purchased Teviotdale from her brother John, who had inherited it from their father with an accompanying 168 acres. Shortly thereafter, she married Charles Dale, an Englishman of "great culture and polish" and began yet another round of home improvements including covering the exterior with stucco, adding the central Palladian window, and elongating the back and side windows in the French fashion, a trend started by Thomas Jefferson at Monticello in 1772.

Upon the depletion of the family's funds, her husband, who was British, tired of America and implored Harriet to return with him to England. Oddly, this move excluded her children, who were left in the care of her brother Henry Walter's widow, known as "Widow Mary" Livingston. Mary's home, originally named Linlithgo, and later called The Hill, was a spectacular Federal house near Teviotdale; it burned to the ground in 1972. Still present are the snapdragons, which she is said to have been the first to import to America.

Back in England and in need of funds, Harriet and Charles Dale mortgaged Teviotdale for 10,000 dollars in 1820, six years before Harriet died, continuing the complicated financial maneuvers associated with the history of the house. In 1833, the Bank of England foreclosed on the unpaid mortgage and the property was sold to another member of the family, Carroll Livingston, who was married to Cornelia Livingston, first cousin of Harriet and daughter of Widow Mary. Carroll, who was involved with several

speculative land transactions at the time, including Forth House, immediately sold Teviotdale on a diminished acreage to Christian Cooper. Cooper had been employed by the family at Moncrief Livingston's nearby gristmills as its first miller and as a footman at Teviotdale. He lived to be 110 years old and eventually divided the property among his three children.

John Ross Delafield, the owner of Montgomery Place in Red Hook, purchased Teviotdale, which was then on a plot of land that had been whittled down to four acres, from Cooper's grandson Frank in 1927. This was intended as a gift for John's second son Richard, whose widow, Margaret, returned it to her father-in-law when her husband died in 1945. John then left Teviotdale boarded up and dormant. Shortly thereafter, he set up Delafield Mansion Corporation, which included in its holdings Montgomery Place and Teviotdale.

The sleeping beauty was forgotten until 1969 when Harrison Cultra and Richard Barker were shown the property while staying at Grasmere as guests of Louise Timpson, the former Duchess of Argyll. Harrison later told the present owner Victor Cornelius that "the trees and foliage were growing so close to the facade that we couldn't even open the shutters." Fifteen thousand dollars bought them a project few would dare to engage. The house was open to the elements and never had any plumbing or electricity.

Harrison and Richard had met in Paris in 1958 while Harrison was studying at L'Ecole des Beaux-Arts and Richard was head of advertising at the *International Herald Tribune*. After ten years in Paris, the two returned to New York City following the 1968 student uprisings in Paris. Harrison began working with decorator Rose Cummings and then formed a partnership with Georgina Fairholme, which lasted until 1974. He went on to develop a highly successful office of his own with clients that included Jacqueline Onassis and local Hudson Valley friends Richard Jenrette and Sam Hall and his wife, Grayson. Richard immediately went to work at the advertising agency Doyle Dane Bernbach.

After a significant amount of structural stabilization, Harrison, assisted by Georgina Fairholme, began the interior decoration of the house. Walter Livingston's order books for the construction of the house are intact and reside at the New-York Historical Society, so much information regarding the original materials was available while the twentieth-century restoration was in progress.

No records of the finishes or details of the decoration existed, except for several bits of remaining wallpaper, leaving Harrison on his own. He reported in *Architectural Digest* that he took ". . . what I considered to be a sensible but imaginative approach. I decided to treat the house as though the long hiatus between its two flowerings had never existed—that one family had been in residence the entire time. I decided that the Livingstons would have been Francophiles, which explains the French Empire furniture. The Fulton era is reflected in the library where I keep a collection of memorabilia

associated with the inventor's life." This includes an 1827 drawing of the house by Fulton's daughter, which illustrates unrealized plans for two symmetrical hyphens, connecting elements leading to octagons on either side of the main block. "I did take liberties, but I felt, in a very real way, that I was entitled to. If you subscribe to my theory of continuity, it was my 'contribution' to the story of the house." One of the "liberties" was the construction of the Chinese Chippendale staircase, whose inspiration and identical predecessor is at Bohemia Manor, the 1745 home of Augustine Herman in Cecil County, Maryland.

Victor Cornelius first arrived at Teviotdale as a guest of Harrison Cultra and Richard Barker in 1979 when the interior decoration had all but been completed. He had started a romantic partnership with Richard Barker, which lasted until Richard's death in 1988. "I could cook, and that suited everyone," says Cornelius. Stored

in the house are the videos he produced in the 1980s documenting oral histories of the occupants of many homes along the Hudson at the time, including Margaret Suckley at Wilderstein, Honoria Livingston McVitty in Sylvan Cottage at Clermont, and Deborah Dows at Southlands. According to Cornelius, "The people I was meeting up here were of a particular sort . . . struggling to stay on their family properties. I went from being the person recording the process to being a part of the process."

Anthony Hail, the decorator from San Francisco, was also visiting that August weekend when Victor first arrived. He remarked on the vibrant crosscurrent that breezes throughout the house when the doors and windows are open in the summer, due to the raised English basement and the position of the house on a hill. Thirty years after Barker's passing, there is an invigorated energy in the home's preservation so that the property, which had dwindled down to four acres, is now inching back in the direction of the original 541 acres. Today, working on a series of land acquisitions and a family trust, Cornelius is adding his own expertise to correct the property's precarious history. The goal is to maintain Teviotdale as a private house. Says Cornelius, "Sure, it could be a museum. It is one of the most historic houses in America that is still in private hands. But am I going to turn it over to the State or make it a not-for-profit? No, sir. And besides, the moment you stop being able to light the fireplaces, the house dies."

OPPOSITE Walter Livingston referred to his bedroom as the "great chamber." Harrison Cultra designed the four-poster bed covered in antelope. ABOVE The yellow bedroom served as a guest room for Martha Washington in the 1790s. FOLLOWING SPREAD A portrait of Lydia Redmond is tucked behind a photograph of Harrison Cultra and Richard Barker from 1980 at the front door of Teviotdale. A painting by Peter Ambrose hangs over the French daybed.

# THE PYNES

## 1790

THE LAND ON WHICH THE PYNES is located in Tivoli has been in the Livingston family, for the most part, since 1766 when Martin Hoffman married Alida Livingston, daughter of Philip, Second Lord of Livingston Manor. Martin inherited the property from his father, Nicholas, who had acquired it in 1724 from the patentee, Pieter Schuyler.

The datestone from the original farmhouse, incised 1761, is located today in the basement of the present dwelling, which is now the home of Nancy Wu Houk and Edwynn Houk. An inscription on the recent foundation references the original stone.

Passing down through family lore is the story that The Pynes, originally known as Green Hill, was spared ruination in October 1777 during the Revolution when the British, under the command of General John Vaughan, continued north on the Hudson River after the burning of Kingston. This was explained in an article that appeared in the November 3, 1777, edition of the *New York Gazette*. Gilbert Robert Livingston, it was maintained, who was loyal to the Crown, protected the property, saving it from destruction by offering the British soldiers wine from his extensive cellar while commiserating with them in a fraternal manner. He sent a messenger to Margaret Beekman Livingston at Clermont with news that the British Redcoats were about to pay her a visit. This bought her time to safeguard her possessions as best she could and escape to Connecticut just before the British burned Clermont as they had planned.

Upon the death of Martin Hoffman's son Anthony, the property was transferred to John Reade, who married into the family

in 1774 when he wed Catherine, a daughter of Robert Gilbert Livingston (Gilbert Robert's brother) of New York City. Reade is most likely the builder of the 1790 house, as evidenced by the formality of the room circulation, scale, and materials, which all point to a post-Revolutionary Federal-era construction. Catherine had inherited significant funds from her father's estate in 1789, which further reinforces the probability that it was not Hoffman who built the house we see today.

Continuing the Gordian knot of familial real estate transactions, in 1794, Catherine and John Reade sold the house to her brother Henry Gilbert Livingston, the youngest son of Robert Gilbert Livingston, and brother of both Robert Gilbert and Gilbert Robert. (The limited nomenclature in each branch of the family begs the question whether they were self-absorbed or just lacking in creativity.) In a further complication, the two brothers were loyalists to the Crown during the Revolutionary War, while the youngest son reinforced his allegiance to the Colonies by becoming a spy, apparently reporting on his brothers' activities. Henry Gilbert added the two lateral wings in 1797. He concurrently built Sunning Hill, now called Callendar House, next door, on speculation, eventually selling it to his cousin Philip H. Livingston.

In an advertisement for the sale of Green Hill dated 1797, Henry described the property as commanding a "beautiful view of the Blue Mountains . . . with a wing on each side connected by a piazza eighty feet long . . . with a smoke house, granary, overseer's house, wash house, and barn . . . all in the best order." The land was verdant with about 200 English cherry, peach, pear, and plum trees. In 1800, Green Hill was sold to Henry's brother, Gilbert Robert, who resided there until 1815 when it was sold as a reduced plot of 200 acres to John Swift Livingston, who renamed the house The Pynes.

A curious explanation for the acreage reduction is that a real estate venture was initiated in 1798. Frenchman Pierre Delabigarre, along with the painter Charles Balthazar Julien Févret de Saint-Mémin, conceptualized a Utopian village, which they called

53

Tivoli, recalling the ruins of Hadrian's Villa outside of Rome. The planned grid of streets included the names Friendship, Peace, Flora, and Chancellor, the last after the principal financial supporter of the project. Delabigarre built his house, the Château de Tivoli, in 1798 on the grounds originally belonging to The Pynes. The house was demolished in 1926 by Roland Livingston Redmond, but the surrounding walls are still the partial perimeter of the present estate, with the foundation now lying under the pool. The venture failed, and Robert "The Chancellor" of Clermont, who lived just to the north, purchased much of the village property upon Delabigarre's death in 1807. Delabigarre removed himself upon the failure of Tivoli and proceeded south to New Orleans where he connected professionally with Edward Livingston, who was himself finding refuge after financial ruin following a messy political situation.

PREVIOUS SPREAD *Action Photo, after Hans Namuth* from *Pictures of Chocolate*, 1997, by Vik Muniz hangs in the dining room, which is furnished with Jacques Adnet pieces. ABOVE The south parlor contains 1940s French furniture, including an Adnet desk and chairs by Marc du Plantier and André Arbus. Between the windows hangs a 1936 photograph by Berenice Abbott. LEFT The Houks' collection of mid-century French furniture continues in the north parlor.

John Swift Livingston inhabited the house until his death in 1867 when it passed to his son Louis, who resided there until 1904. Subsequently Louis, in keeping with family tradition, willed it to his brother, Johnston, who lived next door at Callendar House. Just to the north of The Pynes lies Rose Hill, which was where Louis and Johnston's sister Estelle lived with her husband, John Watts de Peyster. Johnston immediately transferred ownership of The Pynes to his daughter Carola and her husband, Henri, the Count de Laugier-Villars. They are credited with adding the new roofline and retaining the firm of McKim, Mead & White to design and build an additional carriage barn. Thus a family compound of siblings was established along the Hudson at the end of Broadway in Tivoli. In 1925, Roland Livingston Redmond inherited the house from his Aunt Carola, the Countess de Laugier-Villars, who was childless. As he was her favorite nephew, they enjoyed spending time together over the years.

After a series of marriages, the Hawaii-born Lydia Spalding Bodrero Macy di San Faustino found herself the châtelaine of The Pynes in 1962 when she married Roland Redmond. As her attorney, he met Lydia while representing her during her divorce. Roland had four daughters with his first wife, Sara Delano, who had grown up at Steen Valetje, her family's country seat in Red Hook.

Victor Cornelius reminisced about the extravagant party Lydia threw for Roland's eightieth birthday when she hired boats to take guests out on the Hudson and had lunch served by the local Boy Scouts before an evening fireworks display. The event, according to Cornelius, was "the last hurrah before the ebb tide of the old guard in the Hudson Valley turned into a rip tide."

Roland Redmond was the president of The Metropolitan Museum of Art from 1947 until 1964. He was responsible for the loan of Leonardo da Vinci's *Mona Lisa* to the museum in 1963 and the appearance of the *Pietà* by Michelangelo at the New York World's Fair in 1964. He also oversaw the entire funding, design, and construction of the Metropolitan's Grace Rainey Rogers Auditorium as well as the installation of the patio from the Castle of Vélez Blanco. Aileen Mehle, known as the society columnist "Suzy" Knickerbocker, referred to Roland as "very likely the last of the great gentlemen." He maintained a position on the board of the Pierpont Morgan Library and was the recipient of the French Legion of Honor.

In 1987, Countess Edith Macy Schoenborn-Buckheim and her husband, Karl, purchased The Pynes from Edith's mother, Lydia, who then built herself a dower house on the property. The formidable Lydia died in 2010 at the age of 107.

Subsequently, in 1994, Nancy Wu Houk, an art conservator, and her husband Edwynn Houk, who runs the eponymous gallery at 745 Fifth Avenue in New York City specializing in early twentieth-century photography, acquired The Pynes on a thirteen-acre parcel after a closing that lasted the duration of two pregnancies. The north wing holds Nancy's fine art conservation studio, and the south wing contains the kitchen with a processing facility for Nancy's biodynamic honey business, NYBUZZ. The couple removed most of the twentieth-century additions to the house in the early 1990s after moving upstate full-time with their two children and furnished their home with mid-century French furniture and contemporary photography from Edwynn's gallery.

**ABOVE** The majestic cucumber magnolia was planted in the late eighteenth century. **BELOW** NYBUZZ, the biodynamic honey from the apiary at The Pynes is cultivated by Nancy Wu Houk.

# CALLENDAR HOUSE
## 1794

COMMANDING A PARTICULARLY WINNING position on the Hudson River in Tivoli lies Callendar House. The Federal house was built by Henry Gilbert Livingston with the intention of reselling it while he was living on the adjacent property, The Pynes. These types of ventures were a distinct trend in the 1790s, as men of means looked along the Hudson in search of acquiring country seats. Upon completion, the home, on forty-four acres, was immediately sold to Henry Gilbert's cousin, Philip Henry Livingston, a grandson of Philip Livingston, Second Lord of Livingston Manor and a signer of the Declaration of Independence. Philip Henry named the house Sunning Hill and lived there with his wife, Maria Livingston Livingston, from Teviotdale, and their ten children including a son, Livingston Livingston (name redundancy is a Livingston family leitmotif), until May 1828 when he sold it to Robert Livingston Tillotson. The hull of Robert Fulton's steamboat, *North River*, was repaired at the property's mooring in the Hudson, originally home to Hoffman's Ferry, which offered access to the west shore of the river.

Tillotson, who grew up at Linwood in Rhinebeck with his Livingston mother, added to the acreage at Callendar House and enlarged what he called the "neat porch" of 1794 with a colonnade on the west elevation and added a second story to the two lateral wings. He disposed of the property in 1835. Several successive Livingstons followed Tillotson, leading Franklin Delano Roosevelt's esteemed friend and local historian Helen Wilkinson Reynolds, to write in *Dutchess County Doorways*, "In the story of the [Callendar] house, kinship and family association have been an essential factor."

In 1860, the property passed to Johnston Livingston, who, having been raised next door at The Pynes under his father John Swift's

tutelage, was aware of the charms the land held. Johnston started working in 1844 at his cousin Crawford Livingston's express post office in Philadelphia, eventually adding Henry Wells and William Fargo to the company masthead. Together, they specialized in the transport of valuable articles over long distances. In 1850, Johnston formed an association betting on the growth of the New York Central Railroad network, which he named the American Express Company. In 1852, he repeated this process by creating the Wells Fargo Company. With offices rapidly set up in San Francisco, Johnston was indeed a key player in the westward expansion of America. In 1853, while treasurer of the Wells Fargo Company, he married his cousin, Sylvie Livingston, a granddaughter of Widow Mary Livingston of The Hill, located in the Town of Livingston.

Johnston was proud of his Livingston lineage. He purchased the majority of Chancellor Robert Livingston's belongings when the contents of New Clermont, including most of The Chancellor's books and paintings, were auctioned off in 1857. Shortly thereafter, in 1858, he commissioned genealogical research pertaining to the Scottish beginnings of the Livingston name and the titles of the Earldoms of Linlithgow and Callendar, ultimately informing his decision to change his home's name from Sunning Hill to Callendar House in 1860.

Johnston was also the formidable president of the nearby Edgewood Club, founded by the Livingstons to indulge their love of golf and tennis, from 1900 until 1911, the year of his death at age ninety-six. The house was left to his daughter Estelle and her husband Geraldyn Redmond, who were then in the process of building a two-family home in French limestone, designed by McKim, Mead & White at 701 Park Avenue at Sixty-ninth Street with her sister and Tivoli neighbor, Carola, the Countess de Laugier-Villars who had married French aristocrat Henri de Laugier-Villars.

PREVIOUS SPREAD Callendar House is perched upon meticulously terraced lawns. Shown is the south wing, one of a pair designed by Stanford White's firm. ABOVE In the early twentieth-century, the firm modernized the board-and-batten barn with Roman-arched windows. LEFT The pigeonnier is located on the grounds where Franklin Delano Roosevelt proposed marriage to his cousin Eleanor.

This site eventually became the Union Club when the homes were razed in 1931. Estelle and Geraldyn in turn left Callendar House to their son Johnston Livingston Redmond and his wife Kate. Johnston's younger brother Roland eventually moved into The Pynes, upon inheriting it from his Aunt Carola.

The countess soon left her husband, Henri, but maintained residence next door to Callendar House at The Pynes, her family home. The two Livingston sisters, Carola and Estelle, were inseparable in their social and charitable activities. An article in the *New York Sun* from 1913 noted that the sisters were planning a sale at Manhattan's Plaza Hotel's ballroom to benefit St. Sylvia's Cottage Industries in Tivoli.

McKim, Mead & White's improvements to the house, commissioned by Kate and Johnston Redmond, included a large drawing room on the south elevation. Olin Dows, a cousin from nearby Glenburn, was given his first significant commission by Kate Redmond in 1924. Dows, who was twenty years old at the time, decorated this space with owls and fantastic sumac trees sporting blue leaves. The Redmonds' eighty-one-foot yacht, the *de Grasse*, moored at their dock on the Hudson, was visible through the windows of the drawing room contributing to the idyllic setting.

---

**BELOW** Tracy Dows photographed his son Olin at age twenty painting his first significant commission in the drawing room.
**FOLLOWING SPREAD** The 1924 murals depicting owls, squirrels, and sumac trees still grace the walls of the drawing room designed by Stanford White.

Johnston died in 1933 and Kate was remarried in 1940 to William Osborn. She was later influential in generating funds for the preservation and maintenance of Olana, Frederic Edwin Church's Persian palace up the road. Her daughter, Katherine "Doey" and her son-in-law Paul "Lefty" Evans continued the family's tradition of musical chairs by moving into The Pynes and renting it for a period of time in the 1960s.

Kate Redmond resided at Callendar House until 1974. Often, after dinner to entertain guests, she would have her butler bring from the mantel a cigar box filled with bones from a Native American gravesite that had been unintentionally excavated when the back lawn was graded in 1888. The house, which offers both westerly and southerly views, is located in an area that was inhabited by Mahicans until the 1700s; it was believed that on this site the final war between the Mahicans and the Iroquois occurred.

The two partners of the firm Pierre Deux (Pierre Le Vec and Pierre Moulin) purchased the house in 1989. They installed antique Provençal paneling and French limestone mantels, reportedly in homage to the historic French connections of the Livingstons. The present owners, James and Fiona Welch, are working with contractor Michael Pelletier, making adjustments to bring the property into the twenty-first century.

In 1931, Helen Wilkinson Reynolds observed in her book that the succession of households at Callendar House "have maintained it as a gentlemen's country seat and it is characterized by the quiet dignity which accrues to homes where culture and refinement have long held sway." These words speak to the focused attention paid by today's owners toward the renovation of the property.

# OAK HILL

1795

"MARRYING INTO THE LIVINGSTON FAMILY can be painful," Susan Livingston, who owns Oak Hill with her husband, Henry, emphatically reveals. "The beauty of being married to Henry is that he can listen to stories of the Livingston family all day long. When I was young the stories were so boring to me that they really didn't matter, but it can be interesting to trace one's genealogy back to 1036." The couple are sixth cousins, not removed, and of the same generation. Susan explains, "It is amazing to be descended directly from the First Lord, still both have the name of Livingston, and to have fallen in love."

The two met at a Livingston family reunion at Clermont in 1991, and reconnected in Europe when Henry was posted at Credit Suisse and Susan was the managing director of Brown Brothers Harriman in Luxembourg. Several years later, Henry mentioned that his parents, while entertaining Richard Jenrette from Edgewater, had discussed placing Oak Hill in the Town of Livingston on the market. "Well, maybe I should buy it!" was Susan's response. In the blink of an eye, she did just that.

Henry's mother, Maria, was a great-granddaughter of the artist Frederic Edwin Church, whose spectacular Persian-inspired home and studio, Olana, is near Oak Hill. Church built Olana on the highest elevation of his property to take advantage of the magnificent views of the Hudson River and the Catskill Mountains. Maria met her husband, Henry Hopkins Livingston, while visiting family there. Mrs. Church had asked Henry Hopkins if he would row Maria around Olana's romantic lake. The two teenagers eventually fell in love and were married.

Henry and Maria were well known for arriving at events in their 1913 Rolls-Royce dressed in long linen dusters and scarves, which were topped off, respectively, with a touring cap and goggles and a large straw hat and veil. As family friend Squeaky Hatch remembers, when riding in the vehicle, "The bumpy country road might just as well been paved in velvet."

Both Susan's and Henry's fathers were familiar with each other through membership in the Order of Colonial Lords of Manors in America. Susan's father, James Duane Livingston, Jr., assumed the role of Chancellor Robert Livingston during the Order's reenactments of his administering the first presidential oath of office to George Washington. Henry is quoted in a *Connoisseur* article written in 1988 regarding his genealogy, "We can trace our family in Scotland back twelve generations before the first lord of the manor. I don't find that kind of continuity in many other families." In 1974, he gave 200 acres across the Hudson to the National Audubon Society as a sanctuary for geese, eagles, and turkey vultures, which also protected the view from Oak Hill's wisteria-entangled back porch.

Susan and Henry were married in 1997, and around this time acquired the house with 130 acres from his parents. They soon embarked on a series of renovations. Henry is a direct descendant

---

**PREVIOUS SPREAD** Legend has it that John Livingston started construction of Oak Hill in 1793 after he climbed an oak tree on this site and noted the unusual view of the bend in the Hudson River. The Livingston tartan and the Scottish and American flags fly from the front porch. **LEFT** The painting over the library's fireplace by John Sutton illustrates Boston's port where Robert Livingston, the First Lord, first arrived on the *Catherine* from Scotland in 1673.

67

**OPPOSITE** Over the dining room mantel hangs a portrait of Robert, the First Lord, painted in 1718 by Nehemiah Partridge. The Livingston tartan lies on the dining table under famille rose vases. **ABOVE** The portrait by Robert Fulton of the Third Lord Stanhope, a fellow inventor he had met while in Paris, hangs in the gold parlor. In Stanhope's hand is a light-sensitive plate, an early object that contributed to the invention of photography. The Duncan Phyfe pier table is decorated with stenciling and gilding, and was part of a set commissioned in 1820 for Oak Hill.

John Livingston married his first cousin, Catherine "Kitty" Livingston, who had repatriated back to the Livingston territory from Liberty Hall in Elizabethtown, New Jersey, where her father, William, was governor. She and her sisters—Sarah, Mary, Susanna, Judith, and Elizabeth—were considered extremely eligible due to their beauty, wit, and intelligence. The wedding took place at Catherine's sister, Sarah, and her husband John Jay's home in Manhattan, and the couple raised their children at Oak Hill. The Jays and the Livingstons were inseparable; John and Sarah Jay visited Oak Hill often. As an older man, John wore the style of dress popular with courtly gentlemen during his youth—knee breeches, silk stockings, and silver buckles. His long queue was rewound every morning.

At age twenty-nine, Herman, the tenth child of Mary Ann Leroy, inherited the home upon the death of his father, John Livingston, in 1822 along with some 30,000 dollars of debt. John's will conclusively directed the administrator of the document to forfeit the inheritance of any child who contested the will to the benefit of his siblings. Herman's daughter Cornelia Livingston married Clermont Livingston, The Chancellor's grandson, at Oak Hill. Moving a few miles south to Clermont, she became the second woman in this branch of the family entitled to hyphenate her duplicate surnames. It is her son, John Henry, who inherited Clermont in 1895.

In the 1870s, Herman's son Herman Thong added the mansard roof and third floor. He also enlarged the west porch facing the Hudson. He did so with the income generated from Livingston, Fox, and Company, which owned a fleet of ocean liners. During this renovation a collection of family documents disappeared from the house, only to eventually resurface later at a New York City auction. This collection now resides in the Gilder Lehrman Archive at the New-York Historical Society. It consists of letters written in Low Dutch by Robert, First Lord, and his wife, Alida, in the 1680s, which record the difficulties of running what was little more than a colonial trading outpost.

Several "Hermans" later, Susan has "Livingston" entered into eBay to alert her of any historic family items that may make their way to market. Recently the family rented Dundas Castle, which is adjacent to the towns of Linlithgow, Callendar, and Livingston in Scotland. These are all names that have migrated along with the family to Dutchess and Columbia Counties as well. After diligent online research, Susan found the original diary of Reverend John Livingston, the First Lord's father, in a dusty box while in Scotland. In his writings he discusses the tribulations of religious persecution that led him to move to Holland. The American branch of the family wore kilts with the Livingston tartan at dinners during the trip; one of the tartans presently covers Oak Hill's dining room table.

Susan says that she is "influenced by learning from the first Robert's success in the eighteenth century through his use of foreign language and his wife Alida's perseverance. I have some good business genes," referring to the First Lord who immigrated to the British Colonies speaking English and Dutch, and his wife, who expertly ran the manor while he was away. Robert's armoire, or *kaas* in Dutch, which accompanied him in 1763 from Holland, stands in Oak Hill's center hall.

"My job now is to ensure that my family's tenure at Oak Hill will be sustainable for a generation or two," asserts Susan. Their daughter, Julia, age sixteen, is now the fourth female at Oak Hill able to sign her name Livingston-Livingston.

of the builder of Oak Hill, John Livingston; the house has not been sold out of the family for nine generations. Susan and Henry are the last Livingstons, still bearing the surname, to own a piece of the original 1686 Royal Patent.

In 1790, John Livingston's father, Robert, Third Lord of Livingston Manor, had divided his property among his sons into four great lots inland and four smaller lots on the river, following the abolishment of primogeniture in New York State in 1786. John's 28,000-acre portion was centered in what is now the Town of Livingston, then eponymously named Johnstown. Here, he built a house for his first wife, Mary Ann Leroy, who died after the birth of her tenth child, Herman, in 1793. The same year, John sold that home to his brother and mortgaged much of the fourth great lot to finance land development across the Hudson in Athens, then called Esperanza.

Oak Hill was built with the proceeds from the sale of his property across the river on the site of a grove of oak trees. As passed down through family lore, John, after climbing to the top of an oak tree on the property, pronounced that this spot had the best view of the Hudson River. The house was constructed there using locally milled timber from his small lot, situated at the northwest boundary of Livingston Manor where the Wachankassick Creek enters the Hudson. In addition to land investment, John constructed a route that commenced in Salisbury, Connecticut, continued onto Ancram, where the family steelworks were located, then crossed to Oak Hill's dock and across the Hudson, connecting to the Susquehanna Turnpike and enabling the transport of Livingston steel.

WILDERCLIFF

1799

A STORY THAT HAS PASSED DOWN through the Livingston family is that at age forty, Catherine, the last unmarried daughter of Robert "The Judge" Livingston and Margaret Beekman, stood looking out at the Catskills from her parents' house, Clermont, and declared that she was going to marry the first man who crossed the threshold. Whether this was a prophecy or a threat we will never know. The threshold crossing occurred later that summer day in 1788 at Grasmere, a house Catherine's sister Margaret Tillotson had rented from a third sister, Janet Montgomery. The potential suitor was the Reverend Freeborn Garrettson, an eminent Methodist circuit-riding preacher who was using the nearby John Benner house to deliver his fervent and intense sermons.

Garrettson knew Margaret's husband, Thomas Tillotson, from their native Maryland, and was a guest at Grasmere for several weeks while preaching in the area. There might not have been a man with a background more dissimilar to the group he met at his host's home. Used to the simplest of surroundings and with not a materialistic bone in his body, he received no pay for his labors and was familiar with poverty. With such a background, needless to say, he was not the suitor that the family had been waiting for on Catherine's behalf.

---

PREVIOUS SPREAD Wildercliff was built just before the end of the eighteenth century as an understated Federal house. OPPOSITE Historically, visitors were greeted without the benefit of a formal entrance hall. Today one of the four original public rooms on the first floor has been transformed into a foyer. ABOVE The bend in the Hudson River creates a dramatic view from the porch.

To be unmarried at forty years old in the eighteenth century was unusual for a daughter of one of the wealthiest and at the time most politically prestigious families in the country. Even the young General Washington, who was drawn to her, had once asked the tall, stately young lady to dance. Over time, Catherine had many suitors. Her premonition while at Clermont proved prescient, however, and after an extremely long and complex courtship that had included Garrettson being barred from visiting, Catherine's mother, the formidable Margaret Beekman Livingston, granted her blessing for the marriage to occur in 1793. Seemingly there was a connection that withstood the threat of disinheritance and filled a void in each party. Ultimately, the marriage that ensued proved to be a very successful one.

The couple first lived in a humble stone house on fertile farmland that lay to the east, off the river, that Catherine had inherited from her Beekman grandfather. Five years after the wedding, in 1799, she exchanged this property for 160 acres owned by Johannes Van Wagenen on a promontory facing south and west on the Hudson with extraordinary views. The house they built, initially referred to as Traveler's Rest, then Briercliff, was finally named Wildercliff—the anglicized version of the Dutch *wilde* and *klippe* (or Indian cliff), referencing a stone on the property with a carving of a Native American wielding a tomahawk and a peace pipe.

Somewhat alienated from her family as a result of the austere teachings of Methodism, Catherine created a legendarily hospitable atmosphere at Wildercliff, akin to a salon. Conversation on diverse topics that might not be considered proper in other homes took their natural course here. Profound discussions of philosoph-

ical and spiritual subjects were commonplace at meals. Julia Olin, who grew up at Glenburn, described Mrs. Garrettson as "the dignified . . . hostess, with her marked features . . . Her slender foot with its pretty Morocco slipper."

"Moral simplicity" was the aesthetic goal of Reverend Garrettson and his wife while they were planning the design of their home. The dwelling they moved into in October 1799 was a clapboard Federal abode with a gambrel roof. The four rooms downstairs were entered without benefit of a hall and there were several bedrooms on the second floor. A number of small additions and the obligatory south-facing porch toward the river were added during the nineteenth century.

In 1849, ninety-seven-year-old Catherine Garrettson was riding in her carriage to Massena, her brother John's home, to be followed by a visit to her sister-in-law Louise Livingston at Montgomery Place. It was there that she uttered her last words and died. The Garretsons' only daughter, Mary, continued her parents' tradition of hospitality until she passed away in 1879. She was responsible in 1842 for commissioning architect A. J. Davis to design and build the Picturesque schoolhouse on Morton Road, which was then on land the family owned. Wildercliff was temporarily rejoined with earlier landholdings when Robert Suckley, who lived at the adjacent Wilderstein, purchased it upon Mary's death.

In the 1940s, Eugene and Julia Clarkson Hawkins, a Livingston descendant, rented the house. Their grandson Eliot, who now lives at Holcroft, which he inherited from his Aunt Cornelia "Nellie" Livingston Clarkson, fondly remembers summers spent nearby at Southlands, Deborah Dows's equestrian center.

Henry James's biographer Frederick W. Dupee purchased Wildercliff from the Suckleys in 1958 while teaching at Columbia University. Mary McCarthy visited, as did Gore Vidal, who eventually purchased Edgewater to the north, after the seed of villa ownership was planted while a guest of Dupee's.

In 1979, Sam Hall, a writer for the television series *Dark Shadows* and *One Life to Live*, and his wife, Grayson, an actress who played the parapsychologist Dr. Julia Hoffman opposite vampire Barnabas Collins, purchased the house. They asked Harrison Cultra, a close friend and neighbor at Teviotdale, to renovate the interiors. Sam and Grayson had become friendly with Elizabeth Taylor and Richard Burton during the 1962 filming of *The Night of the Iguana* in Puerto Vallarta, Mexico; Grayson earned an Academy Award

**ABOVE** The interiors of the house were updated by Jason Bell for Fareed and Paula Zakaria. **OPPOSITE** The guest bedroom on the second floor is upholstered with a nautically themed toile.

nomination for her role in the movie. The Halls became parental figures for Elizabeth's daughter Liza Todd, who was a sculptor living down the road in Staatsburg. Due to their close relationship, Liza's wedding was held at Wildercliff in 1984. As part of Grayson's negotiations with the Rhinebeck police department to provide security detail for the event, Elizabeth Taylor posed for a portrait with each officer after the wedding.

The property was purchased from the Halls in 2012 by journalist and author Fareed Zakaria and his wife, Paula. After renting a summer home in nearby Millbrook, Fareed found the Wildercliff house listed for sale. The proximity of Rhinebeck Farmers' Market sealed the deal, as Fareed is an avid cook. His love of cooking and entertaining is reflected in the enlargement of the home's kitchen into a combined kitchen-family room, where the family spends a great deal of time. Fareed speaks intimately about his connection to the property and the rich literary history of the region.

The designer Jason Bell was brought on to update the interiors after the structural components of the renovation were completed. The goal for the family was to have an elegant home where they could easily entertain friends and could also live comfortably with their three children.

For most of the year, days start with coffee and tea on the veranda, taking in the view, which has changed little since the eighteenth century. Quite different from most of the Livingston homes on the Hudson, which have a distinctly east-west orientation, here the river bends, creating a southern vista that extends into the far distance. The connection to the Hudson and its moving water is poetically expressed by Zakaria, who notes the lack of twenty-first century additions to the landscape across the river, rendering "a timeless experience full of aesthetics and emotion . . . The opportunity, as an immigrant, to take part in the stewardship of an historic American structure with a legacy of intact ownership is very satisfying. As a political geek, the history of the Livingstons spoke to me as well."

According to Fareed, Fala, Franklin Delano Roosevelt's beloved Scottish terrier, given to the president by Margaret Suckley, who lived next door at Wilderstein, was bred at Wildercliff. When asked how one can verify this claim, Fareed's answer, rare for a journalist, was "Sometimes with poetry, research is not needed."

ABOVE A watercolor by A. J. Davis of the view from Wildercliff in the 1840s. LEFT The Gothic-style children's playhouse was once used as a pool house. OPPOSITE Mary Garrettson commissioned A. J. Davis to design the Gothic schoolhouse built on her property in 1842. Architect Peter Charapko and his wife Katherine have respected the original board-and-batten exterior while transforming the interior into their comfortable residence.

MONTGOMERY PLACE

1805

LOUISE D'AVEZAC DE CASTERA MOREAU DE LASSY was thirty-two when she met Edward Livingston in New Orleans. Born in 1772 in Santo Domingo, she had married Monsieur Louis Moreau at age thirteen and moved for five years to Jamaica where he conducted his business. Widowed at seventeen, she moved back to her family's sugar plantation just before the Battle of Santo Domingo during the 1791 Haitian Revolution. Forced to flee on a moment's notice after her father was killed, she crept with her mother and six-year-old sister through a dense forest and obtained passage to New Orleans with several servants. Louise and her mother were able to insert themselves into a cultivated social circle. It was here in 1804 Louise met Edward Livingston, known as "Beau Ned" as a young man, who had arrived under equally challenging circumstances.

While a representative to Congress for New York State, between 1795 to 1801, Edward, the youngest child of Robert "The Judge" Livingston and Margaret Beekman Livingston, brought arguments against the Alien and Sedition Acts, which sought the expulsion of immigrants and the ability of the government to fine individuals for criticizing the authorities. Edward went on to hold the office of United States Attorney for the District of New York before being appointed mayor of New York in 1801. While Edward was suffering from yellow fever in 1803, a clerk in his employ embezzled tens

of thousands of dollars. Subsequently, Edward resigned as mayor and pledged to cover his subordinate's debts. These events caused him to leave New York in shame and travel to New Orleans in 1804, where he could forge a new identity. His wife of thirteen years, Mary, died that year of scarlet fever, and their three children were left in the custody of his brother John at Massena in Red Hook.

Edward and Louise, his second wife, married in June 1805 at the chapel of the Ursuline Convent in New Orleans. The same year, his sister Janet Livingston Montgomery was putting the final touches on the home she called Château de Montgomery on the Hudson River in the town of Red Hook. This name honored both her brother Robert, the minister to France, and the memory of her husband, Richard Montgomery. A year later, Edward and Louise's daughter, Coralie, was born during an eclipse at Sainte Sophie, their sugar plantation outside New Orleans. "God had given him so fair a daughter that the sun has hid his head," recalled Louise Livingston Hunt. In Louisiana, Edward involved himself with several mostly successful real-estate transactions, entering into politics again in 1822. A hugely gifted attorney, he brilliantly codified the civil laws for Louisiana. He also composed a model penal code acclaimed for its pioneering humanitarian elements.

When Edward was elected senator from Louisiana, the couple moved into Decatur House, designed by Benjamin Latrobe, in Washington, D.C. He was soon appointed secretary of state under Andrew Jackson in 1831. When Edward was given the position of envoy extraordinary and minister plenipotentiary to France, the couple moved to Paris in 1833, following in the footsteps of his brother Robert "The Chancellor" and brother-in-law John Armstrong, both of whom had recently held the position. They were accompanied by their daughter and her new husband, Thomas Barton. Louise and Edward were warmly received by the court of Louis Philippe and his wife, Queen Maria Amalia. Louis Philippe

had been hosted by members of the Livingston family while an exile in America, and he warmly returned their hospitality.

Upon their return after Edward's post concluded, the family moved into Château de Montgomery, which he inherited at the time of his sister Janet's death in 1828, renaming the property Montgomery Place. Janet had originally intended the estate to be left to General Montgomery's Irish nephew, William Jones, then later to Edward's son, Lewis, but both had predeceased her.

Janet Livingston was twenty-nine years old when she met Richard Montgomery. He was eight years her senior and an Irish transplant from Swords, County Dublin, who had sold his captain's commission and sailed for America where he eventually was placed in command of the expedition against Canada. Washington Irving referred to him as "the beau ideal of a soldier." According to Irving's biography *Life of George Washington*, Richard, who died in 1775, was one of the first heroes of the Revolutionary War, offered Janet respite from the monotony of family life at Clermont and the time spent with her grandfather, Henry Beekman, in Rhinebeck. He proposed to her in 1773 and they soon married, providing long-craved companionship for both.

In 1802, at age fifty-nine, Janet sold Grasmere, her previous home, to her sister Johanna in order to facilitate the building of a new

Federal home with fewer melancholy memories. That same year Janet purchased a farm with 242 acres in Red Hook from John Van Benthuysen for 8,250 dollars. She immediately commenced building Château de Montgomery, using architectural plans said to have been procured from her brother, Robert, in France.

Thomas Streatfeild Clarkson, the author of *A Biographical History of Clermont*, described Janet in 1869 as "a woman of rare intellectual attainments and vigor of language in conversation." She became famous for her commercial nurseries and orchards. Governor De-Witt Clinton arranged to transport the remains of Janet's husband, General Richard Montgomery, from Canada down the Hudson in June 1818, forty-three years after his death at the Battle of Quebec. Janet waited alone on the riverfront portico of the house she had named for him and at the appointed time *The Richmond* arrived.

---

**ABOVE** The marble urn in the entrance hall was purchased by Thomas and Coralie Barton. The four plaster bas-reliefs were cast from originals sculpted in 1836 by Bertel Thorvaldsen and represent the four seasons. The uniquely constructed tapering colonettes are unusual for the region and period. **OPPOSITE** A. J. Davis added the sixteen-inch precast crown molding in the entrance hall in the 1860s.

The boat stopped for a moment and Handel's *Dead March* was played shortly thereafter. "Her friends and servants now looked for her; she had fallen to the floor in a swoon." She was overcome with emotion.

Edward passed away in 1836, a year after he and his family had returned to Red Hook from Paris. In 1841 his widow Louise and daughter, Coralie, commissioned the noted architect A. J. Davis to make improvements to the house. He had been introduced to Louise and Coralie by the Donaldsons, who lived across the Saw Kill at their home, Blithewood. While working at Blithewood, landscape designer A. J. (Andrew Jackson) Downing collaborated with architect A. J. Davis–giving birth to the American Romantic movement.

ABOVE The library contains many of General Richard Montgomery's personal effects including his campaign trunk and telescope. Above the mantel mirror hangs an unattributed portrait of Montgomery. The Irish settee originally came from Clermont. LEFT The silhouette of Montgomery hangs on wallpaper that features a pattern from the 1880s. OPPOSITE An overmantel looking glass hangs behind a clock depicting Ceres, the goddess of agriculture. In the 1850s, Louise and Coralie Livingston selected the wallpaper for the parlor.

A. J. Davis worked at Montgomery Place under the title "architectural composer." From 1842 to 1844, he designed the famous North Pavilion (or summer parlor), the west veranda, and the south wing. In 1859, he returned to work with Coralie after she received funds in connection with several of her father's contested New Orleans real estate dealings, permitting her to proceed with building a coach house. In 1863, Davis designed the Corinthian semicircular entrance portico that was inspired by the Temple of Vesta in Tivoli outside of Rome. He also added the roof balustrade, effusive exterior ornamentation, and in 1867, the unusual Swiss Factory Lodge that was built to house millworkers. He continued

PREVIOUS SPREAD Edward Livingston's hat rests beside his cane, which contains a piece of a sapling near George Washington's tomb at Mount Vernon. Edward's bust, sculpted by Ball Hughes, occupies a corner. OPPOSITE Nineteenth-century copies of the Warwick Vase rest above the home's signature tapered colonettes at the dining room's entrance. ABOVE A portrait of Coralie Livingston Barton painted in 1840 by Jacques Amans hangs above four bound volumes on gardening written by A. J. Downing. The books were a gift from his widow, Caroline Downing, in 1853.

to collaborate with Coralie after her marriage to Thomas Barton, until she died in 1873. While A. J. Davis was the leading proponent of the Gothic Revival, or as he termed the style, English Collegiate, the work he completed at Montgomery Place was uncharacteristically in the classical vocabulary that he had publicly eschewed in 1835 upon leaving his partnership with Ithiel Town.

The esteemed horticulturist and commentator on rural taste in America A. J. Downing first visited Montgomery Place in the early 1840s and proclaimed that the property was "second as it is to no seat in America, for its combination of attractions, it has been rather that we were silent—like a devout gazer at the marvelous beauty of the Apollo." He was impressed with the commercial business Janet had maintained, which included orchards and nurseries and a Gothic Revival conservatory designed by Frederick Catherwood in 1839. Peppered along the walks and drives were a series of temples and resting places. The concept of a smooth transition from the interior of the house to wilderness was one espoused by both A. J. Davis and A. J. Downing. At Montgomery Place the innovative North Pavilion looked out upon formal architectural outbuildings to increasingly rustic structures designed by A. J. Davis and on into the forest. Across the dramatic cataract, or waterfall, which traversed the Saw Kill, there was a romantic

bridge constructed with tree trunks and bark. In the lake that was formed by a dam at the top of the waterfall, *Psyche's Boat*, owned by Coralie, navigated the waters with a giant butterfly on the prow.

A. J. Downing acquired his "Natural," "Gardenesque," and "Picturesque" vocabulary from the English proponents of the style, Humphry Repton and John Claudius Loudon. The charms of the Picturesque lay in the irregular effects of controlled wildness, a tension between nature and artifice. He described naturalism as "a complex matrix of decorative and behavioral codes."

In 1841, A. J. Downing published the first significant book on the subject, *A Treatise on the Theory and Practice of Landscape Gardening, Adapted to North America; with a View to the Improvement of Country Residences*, which was followed by revered publications on the subject. From his nurseries down the river in Newburgh, he advised the Livingstons on design and plantings in 1844, providing many specimens that are still observed today on the grounds. In the October 1847 issue of *The Horticulturist*, A. J. Downing led the reader on an extended tour of the grounds at Montgomery Place with rich descriptions of the "Wilderness," "Cataract," and the "Flower Garden." He noted that "Whether the charm lies in the deep and mysterious wood, full of the echo of water spirits . . . or the calm, serene mountains . . . certain it is that there is a spell in the air . . . The hour of sunset is the magical time for the fantasies of the color-genii of these mountains seen from the Pavilion." The pleasure grounds became famous as a result of the publications documenting his contribution.

Eventually A. J. Downing's interests evolved to include architecture. In 1846, he sold his nursery in Newburgh in order to dedicate himself to his writings on landscape and architecture. He found the perfect partner in Calvert Vaux, a formally trained architect whom he had met during an excursion to England. Together they formed Downing and Vaux in 1851.

Hans Jacob Ehlers, who would go on to work on the grounds of Steen Valetje, Ferncliff, and Rokeby, was also consulted in 1849 on the Montgomery Place arboretum, which Coralie's husband, Thomas Barton, whose father had written the first American book on botany, had already commenced.

General John Ross Delafield, a relative of Edward Livingston, inherited the estate in 1921 after a decline in the property's maintenance by the Hunts, Coralie's cousins. The Hunts had spent summers at Montgomery Place since 1847. William Hunt visited in 1852 and met his future wife, Elizabeth Ridgely, there. Following their marriage, they began construction of Ridgely just north of Clermont. General Delafield hired Dwight James Baum, the architect of residences in the historic Riverdale section of the Bronx, to oversee the improvements at Montgomery Place he deemed imperative. His wife Violetta's horticultural library is

presently located off the dining room. She added many features to the grounds, including the herb garden and a hedged room surrounding an elliptical pond.

In 1964, when General John Ross Delafield died, the property was divided, with 51 percent of the Delafield Mansion Corporation left to his surviving son, John White Delafield and his wife, Anita. The remaining 49 percent was left to Margaret, the widow of the general's second son, Richard. Margaret maintained the rights to inhabit the house during the summer months. Her brother-in-law John resided in the house the remainder of the year. Following lunch at Teviotdale in the 1980s, Victor Cornelius, Teviotdale's current owner, drove to Montgomery Place with Margaret and filmed the recounting of her experiences in the house; Walter Cronkite was the film's narrator.

John Dennis Delafield inherited the 385-acre property in 1986 from his father, John White, and sold it that same year to Sleepy Hollow Restorations, which later became Historic Hudson Valley. After two years of restoration, they opened the house and grounds to visitors. In 2016 adjacent Bard College purchased the property, enlarging its campus significantly. The magnificent cataracts of the Saw Kill, still active orchards, and extensive pleasure grounds add to the significance of this esteemed American Romantic country seat.

**ABOVE** The century plant given to Janet by her mother, Margaret Livingston, bloomed in 1873. The public was invited to view this spectacle and tour the grounds of Montgomery Place. The Gothic Revival conservatory, designed by Frederick Catherwood in 1839, later became the site of the family's tennis courts.

---

**OPPOSITE** Designed as a summer parlor, the North Pavilion was intended as an observation point to take in the pleasure grounds and the Hudson River. **ABOVE** Hitchings and Company installed Violetta White Delafield's potting shed in 1929. **RIGHT** A. J. Davis designed the Swiss Factory Lodge in 1867 to house millworkers.

IN 1806, WALTER TRYON LIVINGSTON acquired twenty-two acres that he added to land he had inherited in 1790 from his grandfather Robert, Third Lord of Livingston Manor. Together these holdings totaled 450 acres and were located in Bingham Mills, today, a small hamlet in Livingston. The seller of the small plot, John Richmond, had been the owner of The Hermitage, Walter Tryon's childhood home since 1804. The Richmond family changed the name from The Hermitage to Richmond Manor. The Hermitage was built by Walter Tryon's father, Peter R. Livingston, between 1773 and 1784. The naming of the one-story Georgian house referenced Peter's desire to retreat following his financial downfall due to failing land speculation—a place for a hermit. Although not related to the Richmond family, Walter Tryon inexplicably named his new home Richmond Hill.

The Richmonds came from England with expertise in wool production, which was appreciated by Chancellor Robert Livingston, whose flock of Merino sheep had been a gift from Napoleon and were kept near Richmond Hill. Their skill in breeding and rearing sheep, as well as the shearing, carding, and washing of wool contributed to their financial status. As a result, this increased their ability to purchase large tracts of land and to expand wool production facilities that remained open until the mid-nineteenth century.

With his second wife, Betsy, Walter Tryon moved into the stylish brick Federal farmhouse, Richmond Hill, with their children. Today, the house is basically unchanged, with the exception of a brick service wing added to the back in 1900. The original elliptical fanlights with delicate tracery are still intact as are the stone lintels over the six-over-nine window sashes characteristic of the period.

The couple resided twelve years in the house before exchanging their home with Samuel Ten Broeck, and moving into Ten Broeck's home, The Bouwerie. In 1841, Richmond Hill was inherited by Leonard Ten Broeck, Samuel's nephew, and his wife, Helen Livingston, Walter Tryon's daughter. This union is one of many that illustrates how real estate was retained through Livingston bloodlines in the nineteenth century.

**ABOVE** Richmond Hill's kitchen wing and terrace were added to the back of the house in 1900. **RIGHT** The Federal facade exhibits a pediment above a central projecting pavilion, an architectural feature popular in the first decade of the nineteenth century.

# RICHMOND HILL
## 1807

# ROKEBY

## 1811

ROKEBY STANDS OUT. Very few places I have visited have an equivalent halo of unparralleled character surrounding the history, design, and activities associated with this private home. The same family has owned this property for eleven generations since 1688. It is a source of considerable pride for its members who are descendants of the original owners and still reside in their ancestral home.

When Margaret Livingston Chanler Aldrich passed away in 1963, Rokeby, which had been left to her and nine siblings by her mother in 1875, was placed in a trust for the three grandchildren, as her son had predeceased her. Richard "Ricky" Aldrich and his wife, Ania, live at Rokeby full-time, John Winthrop "Wint" Aldrich and his wife, Tracie, part-time, and Rosalind Aldrich Michahelles, some of the time. Margaret imprinted on her grandchildren the primary importance of invested ownership and care of Rokeby.

In 1790, John Armstrong, Jr., borrowed funds from Robert "The Chancellor" Livingston, the brother of his wife, Alida Livingston, to build The Meadows, on the current site of Bard College's Fisher Center in Annandale-on-Hudson. An early real estate speculator,

---

Armstrong sold The Meadows and built Mill Hill in 1795, the location of the future Blithewood estate, also now on Bard's campus. Warner Richards was the carpenter for these extraordinary Federal homes as well as for Rokeby, Armstrong's third house in the area.

A 1798 letter from Armstrong, playing the real estate seducer, to the representative of his friend Rufus King, describes available property in Red Hook as follows: It "is a farm superior to any I have mentioned. It contains 420 acres, 100 of which is meadowland—220 arable, and the remainder, woods . . . There are upon it two situations for building, somewhat different in character, but equally desirable. The one is on the River and commands a long reach north and south. The other is on still higher ground, and farther removed from water; a fine view of the River . . ." The second location mentioned is where Armstrong eventually built Rokeby in 1811.

Armstrong is known for his celebrated unsigned letters that were privately circulated among the officers of the Continental Army stationed at Newburgh. The letters were intended to stir up rebellion against the Colonial government by the soldiers, who had not received compensation for their services. Although the letters were surreptitiously published in 1783 with provocative intentions, George Washington later exonerated Armstrong of any wrongdoing.

After a brief stay across the Hudson River in Kingston for his children's education, Armstrong moved to Washington, D.C. once he was elected New York State senator in 1800. Thomas Jefferson appointed him minister plenipotentiary to France in 1804, directly following in the footsteps of his brother-in-law, The Chancellor, who had previously held the post. Armstrong assumed his position in the court of Napoleon, who was at the height of his power. The couple arrived in Paris, settling in at 100 Rue de Vaugirard, in time to participate in the coronation of Napoleon and Josephine at Nôtre-Dame de Paris Cathedral. Armstrong was selected on November 16, 1804 (twenty-sixth Brumaire, year thirteen, of the French Republican Calendar) by the artist Jacques-Louis David to pose for his monumental painting of the coronation. "Alida enjoyed visiting the great artist's studio on the two occasions her husband was being painted," wrote William Astor Chanler, Jr., in his lengthy hand-typed manuscript about his ancestor. Alida "was presented to Josephine as well as Napoleon's sisters, the Queen of Naples, and Pauline Bonaparte to complete her initiation into court." Well versed in posing for famous artists, Armstrong later had his portrait painted by Rembrandt Peale when the artist visited Paris in 1808.

While approaching the end of his stay in Paris, Armstrong started a search for a future home in the Hudson River Valley. Alida turned to her sister Margaret Tillotson for help and persuaded her husband that upon his return to America in 1810, his

---

**PREVIOUS SPREAD** The entrance hall was plastered and painted in 2012 to resemble the original marble ashlar decoration. The seventeenth-century Flemish tapestry came from Laura Astor Delano's townhouse. **LEFT** The circular radiator in the dining room was included in Stanford White's 1894 plan. Robert Chanler's 1912 panel *Death of the White Hart* is flanked by portraits of Margaret Chanler Aldrich and Richard Aldrich, painted by Ellen Emmet Rand in the 1930s. **FOLLOWING SPREAD** The reception room's wallpaper was installed in the 1830s. Above the piano hangs an 1825 portrait by Waldo and Jewett of Julia Cutler Ward and her sister Louisa.

**ABOVE LEFT** A folding screen painted by Robert Chanler in 1930 covers the door to the library. **LEFT** Stanford White's 1894 design combines two parlors. He selected the wallpaper and the Greek key-crown molding. Laura Astor was married to Franklin Hughes Delano in this room in 1844. **ABOVE** The drawing room's French windows face the Hudson. Above a bronze bust of Robert Chanler sculpted by Serafim Soudbinine in 1920 hangs a portrait of Margaret Livingston Chanler, painted by William Sergeant Kendall in 1900, which was featured on the cover of the January 1903 issue of *Town & Country*.

"future lay on the North River," the name in the early nineteenth century for the Hudson. Six years of intrigue and deception at court more than satisfied any diplomatic ambitions he once had; Armstrong longed to dwell again in the bucolic valley of the Hudson among relatives and friends.

After traveling back to America, the couple lived at Clermont while building their house, which Armstrong financed through a loan from the Manhattan Bank (later J. P. Morgan Chase Bank). He was obliged to offer financial settlements to the Palatine lease-

holders of the Sipperly, Mohr, Finehout, Feller, and Benner farms, who had cultivated the land since 1712, in order to consolidate a respectable amount of property. The dwelling he constructed had six bedrooms and a steeply hipped roof crowned with a pyramidal monitor. The one-hour calèche ride from Clermont to the construction site to oversee the work was bumpy, cold, and dusty.

The Armstrongs named the property La Bergerie (the sheep-fold), reflecting the French tradition of surrounding homes with pastoral views. This was specifically in recognition of the flock of

Merino sheep Napoleon had sent back to America with the family as a gift. Merinos fared less well in the cold northern climate than in Corsica and Spain, so Alida wrote that she organized "genteel ladies [who] devoted as much time knitting sweaters for Merino lambs as for their children."

James Madison had appointed Armstrong secretary of war in 1813 to assist in the ongoing War of 1812. Following the calamities wrought by the conflict, the tides turned against Armstrong politically when the White House was burned, as he was considered accountable for leaving the capital poorly defended.

In 1818, the Armstrongs' daughter Margaret married William Backhouse Astor, Sr., a son of John Jacob Astor, then considered the wealthiest man in America. John Jacob had followed his brother to England from Germany in 1779, and the two produced musical instruments there. In 1783, he sailed to America to sell his flutes and clarinets. Traveling up the Hudson River, he made the decision to accept fur pelts as payment, and eventually opened a fur

business on the side. As a result of his efforts in pushing his trusted agents to further penetrate the Indian Territories, the American Fur Company was established and became prosperous. Astor went on to finance much of the War of 1812 with the proceeds from his mink and beaver pelts as well as his real estate earnings. While working for his father's business ventures, William Backhouse Astor, Sr., was

---

**PREVIOUS SPREAD** The 1858 octagonal Gothic Revival library, with a faux-bois-painted plaster ceiling, contains General John Armstrong's books. The red Empire armchairs belonged to Armstrong. **ABOVE** Robert Chanler's 1925 portrait of Richard Aldrich hangs in the library vestibule. **OPPOSITE** The red velvet-covered stair rail was installed by Stanford White. A laylight illuminates the hall. The portrait on the left is of Alida Chanler Emmet, painted in 1915 by Wilfrid de Glehn. On the right is a portrait of her husband, Christopher Temple Emmet, with his son, painted by Lydia Field Emmet.

to increase the family's holdings from an estimated twenty million dollars in 1848 to more than one-hundred million dollars in 1875.

Margaret Armstrong Astor's passion was literature and horticulture during the Romantic period. Following her honeymoon with William Backhouse Astor, Sr., in 1818, she asked her father to change the name of the farm to Rokeby, after reading the recently published poem of the same name by Sir Walter Scott. She found similarities between a glen on the property known as Devil's Gorge and the landscape in Scott's poem, which describes Rokeby Park near Greta Bridge in County Durham, England. Her fond associations with her family home begged a more romantic name.

John Jacob Astor offered Armstrong the amount of 50,000 dollars for Rokeby in 1835 to assuage Armstrong's concerns about financially providing for his children upon his death. Following the sale, Armstrong moved to his son Henry Beekman Armstrong's house, Wayside, in the village of Red Hook, to live out his winters until he died 1843.

A path called the Poets' Walk was embellished by the the German landscape gardener Hans Jacob Ehlers in 1849. William

**ABOVE** The Crow Room, with walls painted by Robert Chanler in 1900, depicts Mount Overlook and the Catskill Mountains surrounded by poppies and crows. **LEFT** A 1925 portrait of Elizabeth Winthrop Emmet Morgan by Wilfrid de Glehn hangs in the master bedroom. The Zuber pheasant wallpaper was installed by Stanford White in 1894. **OPPOSITE** The bookcase in this bedroom, with its original 1815 plaster walls, was originally at Sylvania.

Backhouse Astor, Sr.,'s subsequent improvements to the house in the 1850s included the polygonal tower on the west side containing a Gothic Revival library that became his favorite refuge. The house was also re-stuccoed to disguise the underlying materials, and an eighty-foot-long porch was added. Astor's love of reading prompted him in the 1830s to persuade his father, John Jacob, to establish the Astor Library on Lafayette Place in Manhattan. Aided by Joseph Cogswell, a scholar and tutor of his future son-in-law, Samuel Ward, Jr., it eventually evolved into today's New York Public Library. Despite the Astors' desire for public recognition through diverse philanthropic gestures, they were intensely private about their family's financial position. True to the family tradition, Astor disposed of his father's personal and financial records before dying.

The Astors had six surviving children who were brought up at Rokeby: John Jacob III, Laura, Alida, William Backhouse, Jr., Henry, and Emily. The eldest child Emily married Samuel Ward, Jr., in 1838. Their daughter, Margaret "Maddie" Ward, inherited Rokeby in 1875. Samuel Ward, Jr., had grown up in Manhattan at Corner House, which was designed by Isaac Pearson and A. J. Davis at the intersection of Bond Street and Broadway. The house included one of the first private galleries in the city. His father commissioned Thomas Cole's painting series *The Voyage of Life* for this space but died before its completion. Financially constrained, the family was forced to let another patron buy it from Cole. Ward, Jr., who was somewhat of a dandy, had studied with Cole. The location of the Wards' house was part of an established neighborhood in the 1830s that included Lafayette Place, Bond Street, and Broadway, and was where Emily Astor spent her childhood.

Maddie was brought up by her grandparents after her mother died while giving birth to a son in 1841. Her father, Samuel Ward, Jr., was thought to be, even for this family, too eccentric and unfit to parent following his swift remarriage to Medora Grymes. When William Backhouse Astor, Sr., died, he left Rokeby to his granddaughter, Maddie, who had wed John Winthrop Chanler, a New York State congressman and twice-elected sachem of Tammany Hall. They had ten surviving children, born between 1862 and 1874, who inherited the property as tenants in common in 1875 following the premature death of their mother, who had caught a chill when returning from her grandfather's funeral. Her demise was followed by the passing of their father, John Winthrop Chanler, in 1877.

This generation became known as "The Amazing Chanlers." Reduced to eight, they came into their inheritance once they reached the age of twenty-one. The rambunctious Chanlers lived lavishly in an atmosphere replete with reminders of their Beekman and Livingston ancestry. After their guardians shuttered the family's Manhattan residence at 192 Madison Avenue, on the site that became B. Altman & Co., they grew up at Rokeby with only periodic oversight as their guardians remained in the city. Meals were observed to be combative in the extreme as each Chanler volleyed for verbal dominance at the table. Family biographer Lately Thomas describes the commonplace scenes as "monumental disputes and fantastic reconciliations."

The eldest sibling, John "Archie" Armstrong Chanler, married Amelie Rives, the "Siren of Virginia," whose temperament was described by the press as "molten lava." Following her success writing *The Quick or the Dead?*, Archie was incarcerated at Bloomingdale Insane Asylum in White Plains by his brothers for his erratic behavior.

In 1886 Winthrop Astor Chanler married Margaret "Daisy" Terry, who had grown up in the Odescalchi Palace in Rome. Their daughter Laura married Lawrence, the son of architect and family friend Stanford White, in 1916.

Elizabeth spent years wearing back braces before breaking free from her chrysalis to emerge as a spectacular beauty immortalized by John Singer Sargent in 1893 while she was visiting London. Her sister Margaret overheard Sargent explaining to Elizabeth during one of the sittings, "Miss Chanler, I have painted you *la penserosa*. I should like to begin all over again and paint you *l'allegra*." While in London, she omitted her imperative curtsey while being presented to Queen Victoria, causing a scandal. Known as "Queen Bess" by her siblings, she married John Jay Chapman, the essayist, and moved into Edgewater.

William Astor Chanler was a congressman and African safari explorer. Upon dropping out of Harvard University in 1888, he embarked on a dhow from Zanzibar to Kenya, and proceeded up the slopes of Mount Kilimanjaro with 120 porters.

On a subsequent expedition he discovered what became known as Chanler's Falls, in present-day Kenya. Described by his sister-in-law Margaret Terry Chanler as "the most promising of the four brothers, he was a brilliant creature, dark-eyed, romantic-looking, with a great personal charm and flawless courage."

Lewis Stuyvesant Chanler served as lieutenant governor of New York State, and was nominated as the Democratic candidate for governor in 1908. He married Alice Chamberlain from Maizeland, in Red Hook, and then wed Julia Olin, who had grown up at Glenburn.

Margaret Livingston Chanler Aldrich became a nurse during the Spanish-American War and an activist in the woman's suffrage movement. She wrote of participating in twelve political campaigns on behalf of three brothers. Margaret married Richard Aldrich, the music critic for the *New York Times*, in 1906 when she was thirty-five years old after obtaining sole interest of Rokeby from her siblings.

Robert Winthrop Chanler was an accomplished artist. His work is exhibited at Rokeby, and he installed his surreal fireplace, composed of bronze and plaster flames, in the former studio of Gertrude Vanderbilt Whitney on Eighth Street in Manhattan. He hosted some of the most riotous parties in New York City, and was the godfather of fashion legend Diana Vreeland. In an article written about Robert in the *New York Sun* in 1912, his home and studio was described in detail: The studio, which was referred to as "The House of Fantasy," was full of live spider monkeys, toucans, ravens, rattlesnakes, and a guyneet cat "with a head like a leopard and nostrils like a weasel." His greatest catch, however, was Harry Thaw, who was committed to Robert's care during his tenure as "Sheriff Bob" for safekeeping during his employ as Dutchess County Sheriff. In 1906, Thaw approached Stanford White at Madison Square Garden and he shot him in a fit of jealousy, avenging White's affair with his wife, Evelyn.

Robert first married Julia Chamberlain, the sister of his brother Lewis's first wife, Alice. He hired the architectural firm Warren & Wetmore to design the couple a French Provincial home but Julia had no desire to live in Red Hook. Robert's second wife, Natalina "Lina" Cavalieri, one of the most famous opera singers and beauties of the time, was to become the inspiration for designer Piero Fornasetti. She orchestrated an advantageous prenuptial agreement with Robert, then quickly divorced him. Upon hearing of the

divorce, his brother Archie Chanler famously sent him a cable that read, "Who's loony now?"—payback for the years Archie had spent in an insane asylum after his brothers had him committed.

The youngest sibling, Alida, married Temple Emmet and lived at The Mallows, their home designed by Charles A. Platt in Stony Brook, Long Island. Before she died in 1969 at age ninety-seven, Alida was the last surviving member of the celebrated "Four Hundred"—the name coined by her cousin Ward McAllister for his list of chosen members of society.

Stanford White, being a close friend of the Chanler family, embarked on sprucing up Rokeby in 1894. White pledged to Margaret that he would "cut about a dozen doors, add some bathrooms, throw a north gable where the attic is, and you will find living here much easier." Armed with a budget of 10,000 dollars, he helped Margaret, who was then twenty-four years old, address inherent issues with the heating, plumbing, and electricity. Among these improvements were the laylight above the central block of the house, the staircase that included two discreet passageways for staff, and

———

The former Rokeby dairy barn has been transformed into a puppet studio for the Professional Arts Workshop, operated by Sophia Michahelles and Alex Kahn.

the combination of two parlors on the west side of the house into a grand drawing room. Still intact in this room is the wallpaper chosen by White as well as his Greek key molding. Margaret held White to the agreed-upon budget even though the final bill for the alterations came to much more. Modifications to the exterior of the house were implemented later by Margaret, who engaged her brother-in-law, the architect Chester Aldrich, of the firm Delano & Aldrich. The firm of Olmsted Brothers was enlisted in 1911 to enhance the earlier 1840s landscape design by Hans Jacob Ehlers.

Today, Shoving Leopard Farm, a cut-flower business run by Marina, Rosalind Aldrich Michahelles's daughter, maintains Rokeby's fertile land that historically was planted with corn by the Lenni Lenape tribe, native to the area. Marina's sister, Sophia, runs a workshop on the property specializing in the production of the puppets that populate Rhinebeck's annual winter Sinterklass festivities as well as New York City's Halloween parade.

"It is hugely gratifying to us that with good luck and hard work, Rokeby is in good shape—the future looks promising," says Wint Aldrich. When considered along with the following quotation from his grandmother Margaret Chanler Aldrich, the stage is set for the present. "Well into this generation of my children, nieces, and nephews, as well as our grandchildren, Rokeby continues to know 'share and share alike.'"

EDGEWATER

1825

BEGINNING WITH THE *COUP DE FOUDRE* experienced upon his first seductive glance of Edgewater, Richard Jenrette, who sadly passed away in 2018, has written extensively about his home. There was an element of the mystical and preordained apparent when listening to Jenrette recall the myriad coincidences and fortuitous serendipities that led to his stewardship of this property. These circumstances have been instrumental in furnishing the interiors with period pieces, many original to the house.

In 1969, Jenrette and his partner, Bill Thompson, were exploring the area with a copy of *Historic Houses of the Hudson Valley* by Eberlein and Hubbard in hand. Trespassing, as only the most fervent architecture aficionados would have the courage to do, they walked around the property, taking in the unique composition of the land and residence. On their return to New York City that evening, the first of many providential telephone calls came through. This one was from Anthony Hail, the San Francisco decorator who had worked on Jenrette's house at One Sutton Place in Manhattan. He was in Rome and had just spent the day with Gore Vidal, who was living there at the time. Vidal, it appears, was a breath away from placing his home Edgewater on the market. A quick sale in 1969 of the house on close to five acres was made to Jenrette for 125,000 dollars. The coveted treasure was captured.

The land on which Edgewater was built was a gift in 1824 from John R. Livingston to his daughter Margaret in celebration of her marriage to Lowndes Brown in 1819. The site, echoed in the current name of the house, was extremely close to the Hudson River in Barrytown and had been Margaret's favorite spot while growing up at her father's estate, Massena. In 1812, Washington Irving, then age twenty-nine, had accompanied young Margaret to Edgewater's future site and had commented favorably on the magnificent view.

The plan of the 1825 house is unusual for the area. There is strong speculation that Charleston native Lowndes Brown had access to Robert Mills, the city's leading architect at the time, and enlisted the popular designer to lend an eye to the project. Several details point to this; chief among them are the proportions of the round-headed French doors on the Hudson River side of the house and the tripartite end windows. Mills had built many public structures in the classical idiom, but Sylvania, as Margaret had originally named her house, is an early adaptation on the temple form incorporated into a residential design that anticipates the 1830s Greek Revival. The monumental hexastyle two-story portico facing the river references Palladio's Villa Foscari, known as "La Malcontenta" on the Brenta River in Italy. The undulating lawn terraces added later obscure the high podium on which the house sits. Jenrette reacted to this comparison, proclaiming "If Edgewater is not quite as grand as 'Malcontenta,' the Brenta is no match for the mighty Hudson."

The Browns happily occupied the house until 1851 when the advent of the Hudson River Railroad, which connected Manhattan to Albany by following the coastline of the river, imposed itself

through the property. This created for almost all the Livingstons who lived on the river a sensory assault, as the trains ran past most of their homes. None was more affected than that of Margaret, whose front door was a scant fifty feet from the track. The railroad company, having seized this conduit by eminent domain, left her with a sword of Damocles hanging over Edgewater. Repulsed by the belching soot that was a necessary by-product of nineteenth-century trains, and in mourning for the recent loss of her husband, Margaret packed her bags and left for England, never to return again.

Despite the intrusive nature of the train, Robert Donaldson and his wife, Susan Jane Gaston, jumped at the opportunity to purchase the Browns' country seat on February 3, 1853 for 22,500 dollars. At age twenty-one, Donaldson inherited 300,000 dollars from a bachelor uncle in London, purchased the property, and immediately changed the name of the house from Sylvania to River Lawn, and then later to Edgewater. Unsure whether he would build another home on the Edgewater property or subdivide it, he sold his estate, Blithewood, which was a fifteen-minute carriage ride to the north, to John Bard for triple the price he had negotiated with Margaret Brown's attorney for his new home.

During his first sail up the Hudson in 1818, Donaldson had written that he "thought it the consummation of earthly bliss to live in one of those pallaces [sic] on such a noble river." In 1835, he purchased ninety-five acres from John Cruger. In conceptualizing the house he would call Blithewood, Donaldson had engaged the services of architect A. J. Davis and landscape designer A. J. Downing. Accomplishing what he had set out to achieve at Blithewood may have been the impetus that led him to look for another project, prompting him to buy Edgewater. Originally planning to build one of A. J. Davis's romantic villas up on the hill far from the train tracks, Donaldson instead settled into the Browns' house with ideas brewing.

---

**ABOVE** The verre églomisé portraits include several members of the Livingston family, including Margaret, the first owner.
**OPPOSITE** The reception room is painted in the original vivid red from the 1850s. Susan Gaston Donaldson's 1832 portrait, painted by George Cooke, hangs next to a harp, which is also depicted in the painting. The suite of Duncan Phyfe furniture was commissioned by Robert Donaldson.

**ABOVE** An 1821 painting of Robert Donaldson by Charles Robert Leslie hangs in the dining room above the sideboard. On the far wall are Gilbert Stuart portraits of Marcia Burnes Van Ness and her husband General John Peter Van Ness. The suite of twelve Duncan Phyfe dining room chairs are dated 1820; they descended through the family of Goodhue Livingston. **OPPOSITE** The chariot clock acquired by Richard Jenrette in England is identical to one purchased by Robert Donaldson in 1821.

A. J. Davis shortly thereafter added improvements to Donaldson's new home at Edgewater. An extremely long enfilade was created with the addition of what Donaldson referred to as an "elegant and commodious" picture room and library connected by a small hyphen on the north, balanced on the south elevation with a walk-in bay window. This window shape was newly introduced at the time and permitted maximum opportunity for appreciating the changing views of the Hudson River, something Jenrette always took full advantage of when in residence while eating his breakfast.

The library, referred to Donaldson and Vidal by its Latin name *sanctum sanctorum*, is crowned with a lantern, or skylight, and has two doors, "one to be glazed with a plate of glass with a stained-glass border, and the other towards the railroad to be glazed with porcelain plates." In 1866, an article appeared in a local newspaper describing the library: "This portion of the building is octagonal in form and the books and gems of art are arranged after the style of the Vatican at Rome."

The exterior of the house was covered in stucco, which was scored and painted to represent ashlar marble. A. J. Davis was also responsible for designing the two complementary gatehouses that face each other along the original approach to the house. To the south of the dining room he added a boathouse with a chinoiserie roofline. Donaldson earned the Latin sobriquet "Arbiter elegantiarum" from A. J. Downing for his talent in creating spectacular and historically important environments for himself and his family.

Donaldson's tenure ended in 1872 when he died and was buried at Sylvania Chapel on the property. The house passed to his daughter Eliza, who in turn left it to her sister, Isabel. It was Isabel

who eventually sold off the furniture and paintings from the house in order to generate income.

In 1902, Elizabeth Chanler, one of the eight "Astor orphans," then married to the writer John Jay Chapman, a descendant of Chief Justice John Jay, purchased Edgewater on 253 acres from Isabel Donaldson Bronson for 40,000 dollars. Chapman penned several of his brilliant writings in A. J. Davis's Octagon Library. Their new home, designed by Charles A. Platt to offer a more comfortable environment, was located up on the hill far away from the train tracks. This house they called Sylvania in homage to Edgewater's previous name. Vidal later noted that Chapman was "easily the most original of American essayists." Edgewater was sold on much reduced acreage to Chapman's son Conrad in 1917.

After languishing for several decades the house was purchased in 1950 by Gore Vidal, who, at age twenty-four, was shown the house by Alice Astor Pleydell-Bouverie while a guest at her nearby home, Marienruh. He immediately acquired the house and property for 16,000 dollars. Vidal had published *The City and the Pillar* in 1948, which describes the coming of age of a young man discovering his homosexuality. He wrote *Myra Breckenridge* in the Octagon Library and in fact credits the evolution of his writing to his environment on the river. "When a writer moves into the house that he most wants or needs, the result is often a sudden release of new energy . . . the result of the Octagon Library?" Apparently the room, as muse, had seduced him into an intense period of reading Petronius, Apuleius, Henry James, and Walter Scott. He used the proceeds from *The Judgment of Paris*, the first book he wrote on-site, for improvements to the house. A small literary circle had blossomed in the area that included Mary McCarthy, Saul Bellow, and F. W. Dupee, who lived nearby at Wildercliff. Paul Newman and Joanne Woodward were frequent visitors, as were Honoria Livingston and Rex McVitty from Clermont, Norman Mailer, Lionel and Diana Trilling, and Eleanor Roosevelt. Dinners co-hosted with his partner Howard Austen would often be punctuated by the whistle of the passing train, but Vidal had mastered the schedule, enabling him to turn the conversation to new guests immediately preceding the arrival of the intrusion, and thereby completely drowning out any possible response. Edgewater was Vidal's base when he ran for Congress in his local district on the Democratic ticket in 1960.

When Jenrette had first viewed the property in 1969, he had no idea at the time of how the history of the house would be intertwined with his own life, until he began to research the lineage of ownership and discovered the name Donaldson on the deeds. At the time, his company Donaldson, Lufkin & Jenrette was a successful investment firm. His partner William Donaldson, although not a blood relative of Edgewater's previous owner, offered a prescient indication of the subsequent coincidences to come.

Aided by a group of friends who became known as the "Empire Mafia," Jenrette painstakingly researched, located, and reintroduced dozens of items from the Livingston family back into the house, their place of origin. The friends assisting and sometimes competing with him on these treasures included Edward Vason Jones, who had served as "architect of the White House"; Berry Tracy, curator of the American Wing at The Metropolitan Museum of Art; Fred J. Johnston, an antiques dealer in nearby Kingston, who was special advisor to Henry DuPont; and Dick Button, the renowned figure skater.

Harrison Cultra, then the owner of Teviotdale, called early on, announcing to Jenrette, "Your lady is in the current issue of *Antiques Magazine* [*The Magazine Antiques*]!" Cultra was referring to a photograph of an 1830s portrait that depicts Mary Donaldson with her harp. That portrait now hangs in the red room next to the same harp depicted in the painting. The suite of furniture, also illustrated in the painting, was designed for Mrs. Donaldson by Duncan Phyfe. A Grecian-style sofa, discovered at Sotheby's, was later attributed to Phyfe, although uncharacteristic of his work at the time. One conjecture is that Donaldson, who was in London in 1820 to collect his inheritance, had visited Thomas Hope's home on Duchess Street and imported his findings, which influenced Phyfe.

Despite having five children, there was only one living Donaldson descendant surviving in the 1970s—Mary Allison, a great-granddaughter of Robert and Susan. It was discovered through a chance encounter with one of Jenrette's fraternity brothers during a college reunion that she lived in Spain. Jenrette was able to arrange a visit with her and her husband, Ivor. Upon entering the Allisons' home, Jenrette spotted a portrait of Robert Donaldson, painted in 1821 by Charles R. Leslie, while he was collecting his inheritance in London. The trove of pieces at the Allisons' with Edgewater associations was encyclopedic. The two developed a shared interest over many years of transatlantic correspondence, which eventually led to Mary designating transfer of the Donaldson items in her will to Jenrette. Returned back to Barrytown were several portraits, including that of Robert Donaldson, a magnificent mahogany wine cellarette, chairs, silver, photographs, and manuscripts, most of which are listed in the home's 1872 inventory.

In 1998 Michael Pelletier built guest and pool houses that had been designed by Michael Dwyer. These additions paid homage to the tradition of early nineteenth-century estates with dependencies. One hundred and fifty acres were purchased across the Hudson and placed in land conservancy to protect the viewshed.

Richard Jenrette established Classical American Homes Preservation Trust in 1993. His inspiration was Frances Edmonds and the Historic Charleston Foundation, where he had joined the board after purchasing Roper House, a Greek Revival residence from 1838 on the High Battery in Charleston. His other five houses are examples of classical American architectural design from the eighteenth through the twentieth centuries. Eventually all of these dwellings will be included in the trust. In discussing the formation of the trust with Jenrette, he explained that it was put in place to protect the residences—his vehicle for self expression—in perpetuity. A house can be sold or left to an heir. Absent an heir, he wondered, "What was I going to do with all these houses?" As exemplified at Edgewater, Jenrette has created environments with these homes that occupy an otherworldly realm, balancing the past with the present.

---

# GRASMERE
## 1828

THE LINEAGE OF OWNERSHIP AT GRASMERE might best have been served with a revolving door. While many of the family homes along the Hudson became tied to one branch of the Livingston family, Grasmere has served many and been tied to none.

Janet Livingston Montgomery started construction of an earlier incarnation of Grasmere with her husband, General Richard Montgomery, in 1773. The house was situated on 618 acres left to her by her grandfather Henry Beekman, just south of Rhinebeck Village. Janet's sister Margaret and her husband, Thomas Tillotson, a New York state senator, had resided at Grasmere right before they moved into their newly finished home, Linwood, in 1790. During the Tillotsons' stay at Grasmere, Catherine, another Livington sister came for a visit. At that time, the Reverend Freeborn Garrettson was also a guest and the two were introduced. They eventually wed and began construction of their home, Wildercliff. Following the Tillotsons' stay at Rhinebeck House, as Grasmere was then called, the house was rented to Lady Kitty Duer, the daughter of William, Lord Stirling, in the 1770s. Her son William Alexander Duer was born here in 1780, and later became the president of Columbia College.

Grasmere developed a reputation within the family as a refuge for members to use while building more ambitious residences in the area. In the 1790s, the large brick house was rented by a third sister, Gertrude, and her husband Morgan Lewis, the future governor of New York State, while construction of their home, Staatsburgh House, was underway.

In 1802, Grasmere was sold to Janet's sister Johanna and her husband and cousin, Peter R. Livingston. It was this couple who in 1828 rebuilt the house on the footprint of the original structure after a devastating fire in 1824. Johanna and Peter had no children, so Grasmere was gifted to Johanna's nephew Maturin and his wife, Margaret Lewis Livingston. When Margaret Lewis Livingston inherited Staatsburgh House from her father in 1844, the couple gave Grasmere to their son Lewis, who shared tenancy with his brother Robert James in 1850.

Lewis added the arched tops to the windows on the first floor and the front porch to the Georgian-style house. Hanging in the entrance hall were three Gobelins tapestries, which had been procured by his cousin Johnston at the sale of Robert "The Chancellor" Livingston's effects at New Clermont in 1857. In 1860 Lewis inherited an additional 280 acres, increasing the property to an impressive 898 acres.

In 1894, Henry and Sarah Minerva Schieffelin were looking for a place to discreetly set up house for their daughter, Fanny, and her husband of seven years, attorney-poet Ernest Crosby. Grasmere fit the bill perfectly. Although from superlative stock, Ernest was fond of espousing progressive ideas that were anathema to polite society of the time. His father-in-law had called in a favor from his friend President Benjamin Harrison, who posted Ernest in Alexandria, Egypt, as a judge in the Mixed Tribunals, a lifelong appointment that adjudicated grievances between foreigners and Egyptians. Not finding this position to his liking, Ernest quickly sent his wife and two children back to New York City and embarked for Russia in order to meet Tolstoy, a writer whose feelings for the underclass resonated with his own. His in-laws decided that enough was enough after he invited Russian socialist Maxim Gorky to their house at 665 Fifth Avenue, and that if he was installed in Rhinebeck ". . . he wouldn't be able to bring such politically volatile acquaintances home for dinner."

ABOVE AND BELOW Three views of the interior of Grasmere include the entrance hall, one of several classical Italian marble mantels in the house, and the service stairs. OPPOSITE The elaborate stone barns and stables were constructed by the Crosbys at the beginning of the twentieth century.

Ernest and Fanny made several improvements to Grasmere. They transformed the entrance piazza from wood to marble, and added a series of formal Italian gardens. An enormous stone barn was constructed in 1901. On the farm, cows and pigs were bred. Pear and apple trees were cultivated for the family's table. A pair of gatehouses in the English Lake District style were built at the carriageway's entrance, which was planted with locust trees by Janet Livingston Montgomery in the 1770s. As a young boy, their son, Maunsell Crosby, spent his free time developing an expertise in ornithology. With his tutor, he traversed the property's fields that had names such as North Buccobush, Fifty Acre, and Foxhollow in search of birds. Maunsell became famous for his birding weekends when he would invite fellow ornithologists to explore and catalog the local offerings. One such guest was his neighbor Franklin Delano Roosevelt, who kept Maunsell's portrait on his fireplace mantel at Hyde Park.

When Maunsell died in 1931, his nineteen-year-old daughter, Helen Crosby, inherited Grasmere, but she had not a cent to maintain it. Until the will was reversed and a trust established, Helen took in paying guests while finishing up her studies at Vassar College. When she died, she left a trove of letters and diaries with a note to her daughters that began ". . . to read after I am gone. In these papers you will find answers to the questions I know you have had." One of the daughters, Susan Gillotti, wrote about her findings in her book *Women of Privilege*, chronicling the Crosbys' life

at Grasmere and their time spent at the Edgewood Club of Tivoli playing lawn tennis. Under the ownership of the Crosbys, the house was leased by the Foxhollow School for girls from 1935 until 1939 before being sold to Allan Ryan, owner of nearby Ankony Farm. Lillie Havemeyer made Grasmere her residence in 1939 following Ryan's brief ownership.

In 1955, Robert Clermont Livingston Timpson, a grandson of John Henry from Clermont, reinstated the Livingston name into the line of Grasmere's ownership. His wife, Louise, the former Duchess of Argyll, became great friends with the decorator Harrison Cultra. It was when renting the second floor at Grasmere in the late 1960s that Louise showed him Teviotdale while touring the area. When this historic house became available in 1971, Cultra purchased it.

During a short-lived experiment in communal living beginning in 1972, Grasmere was bought by a group of six couples from New York City who divided up the living quarters. Dinner was served communally, but the couples maintained their own separate living spaces for the remainder of the day.

Jonathan Mensch, the present owner, is currently planning to refurbish the property to become an inn, which will include a culinary center in the barn complex as well as twelve guest rooms in the main house and eco-guest cottages nestled into the surrounding fields. The intention is to keep the property and its history intact. Perhaps there will be a new kind of revolving door at Grasmere.

# FORTH HOUSE

## 1835

MY FIRST VISIT TO FORTH HOUSE in the Town of Livingston was with my son, Elio, who was three years old at the time. This marked the first step into my search for a country home in the area, which would bring me before more than one hundred houses. Forth House is the one that got away, but all is well that ends well. The gentlemen who were truly ready to make the purchase, Jim Joseph and Scott Frankel, the present owners, have become dear friends. Elio and I often visit and observe the pitch-perfect renovation of the home and its flawless grounds.

This 1835 Greek Revival brick house is closer in design to urban homes in New York City and Boston of the time than to the plethora of even the most high-style rural residences constructed during the 1830s. The quality of interior ornamentation found here is rarely seen in country houses of this period.

There was a great deal of empathy in America for the plight of the Greeks in their quest for independence ending in 1832. At the time, cultured Europeans explored ancient Athens and a design vocabulary of refined classicism ensued. The juxtaposition of the gravitas of the Doric order's simplicity with the fluidity of such features of Greek ornamentation as the anthemion, paterae, and acanthus created a style popular in the United States well into the 1840s.

———

PREVIOUS SPREAD The west facade of Forth House, with its hipped roof and original Ionic portico, sits at the end of an elliptical drive that is punctuated with weeping beech trees. OPPOSITE The hemlock allée was planted in the 1970s. ABOVE Classical Greek design elements, including the anthemion and simulated bronze nailheads, decorate the front entrance door.

Forth House was named for the Firth of Forth, the estuary of several rivers, including River Forth, outside Edinburgh in the Livingstons' ancestral home, Scotland. Forth House's property is composed of the southernmost of four land inheritances that in 1790 passed down from the Third and last Lord of Livingston Manor. The name Forth is also a *jeu de mots* representing both geographical heritage and the pecking order among the sons. The land on which Carroll Livingston built his house was divided from his cousin John's house directly to the north.

Carroll Livingston, a son of U. S. Supreme Court Justice Henry Brockholst Livingston and great-grandson of Philip, Second Lord of Livingston Manor, purchased land from several smaller Livingston landowners in 1832, including the land divided off from John's neighboring acreage.

Carroll's extremely sophisticated interpretation of the Greek Revival style displays a floor plan that mirrors, on a slightly diminished scale, Montgomery Place nearby. He accomplished this on the footprint of a previous eighteenth-century brick home, which may explain the fact that there are only three bays for such a wide front elevation. The staircase is tucked into its own room off the main hall to the right as one enters Forth House, and to the left at Montgomery Place. There is an identical bifurcation at the end of the entrance hall in both houses, where guests can choose to continue into the dining room on the left or the parlor on the right. The two connected rooms feature guillotine windows; befitting their name, once the sashes are raised, the space overhead is wide enough for a tall man to pass through onto the veranda. A window sash would often become unsteady and fall down with the inevitable tragic results.

The extraordinary details at Forth House elevate the visitor's experience. Lead paterae surrounding the window and door moldings date to 1835. The exuberant anthemion carving over the front entrance is punctuated by columns in the Ionic order. Further academic and archaeological research conducted in Greece at the beginning of the nineteenth century led to other architectural references that we see exhibited throughout the house—from the medallions, inspired by those from the Erectheum on the Acropolis, to the doors, which are based on the early nineteenth-century drawings of Minard Lafever depicting the Treasury of Artemis. The design elements illustrated in the decoration of the house include honeysuckle, representing hospitality, and swirling acanthus leaves, representing immortality.

Carroll Livingston's abbreviated tenure at Forth House ended in 1840, when the house on ninety-five acres was sold to Russell Forsyth for 14,000 dollars. This seems to have been prompted by the fact that Carroll and Cornelia had separated. Cornelia left for France with her two children to live near her sister-in-law Caroline de Grasse de Pau Livingston. Eventually she moved to Staten Island to be closer to her sister Ann and brother-in-law Anson Livingston. Carroll ended his legal career in compromised circumstances as a

---

**ABOVE** The carpet in the entrance hall came with the house. The bifurcation at the end of the hall is reminiscent of that at Montgomery Place. **OPPOSITE** A classical Boston mirror hangs between two windows with original unpainted lead paterae incorporated into the Greek Revival trim of the library. A large section of ingrain carpeting from the 1850s covers the floor.

boarder. Cornelia's census report from 1848 showed her superior financial situation in comparison to her estranged husband.

Forsyth transferred ownership of the house on 330 acres in 1855 to Adam and German Finger for 33,000 dollars. They maintained residence there until 1858, when they sold it to Robert McLane on a reduced sixty-nine-acre plot for 14,000 dollars. McLane was to become governor of Maryland and American ambassador to France. It was shortly after Robert's employ in France, which lasted from 1865 until 1874, that the house was rented to Henry Walter Livingston III, Carroll's nephew, and his wife, Angelica, before they inherited The Hill from his father.

Several owners later, in 1959, the Van Dyke family purchased the property. Two bachelor sons, Harry and his brother, Frank, along with their mother, Clara, worked to restore the house over a period of forty years. Harry, an architect who worked with industrial designer Raymond Loewy, was responsible for the addition to The Frick Collection in New York prior to designing the conservatory at Forth House in 1980. This room has now been transformed into a spacious kitchen and gathering room.

Jim Joseph, an architect based in New York City and his partner Scott Frankel, the composer for the Broadway musicals *Grey Gardens* and *War Paint*, purchased Forth House in 2004 after renting a house two miles away. "So much needed attention, but the original detail survived intact," Jim recalls. The two men have

---

PREVIOUS SPREAD In the living room, a 1940s French wallpaper panel hangs above the Blüthner piano. The carriage clock on the mantel once belonged to Katharine Graham. LEFT On the right wall of the dining room is a painting by Frank Faulkner. The 1830s chairs were made by Joseph Meeks & Sons of New York. ABOVE The hyphen connecting the kitchen to the dining room serves as a bar.

OPPOSITE The striped carpet in the stair hall adds a graphic counterpoint to the nineteenth-century floral wallpaper. ABOVE LEFT AND RIGHT Unique door details and nineteenth-century silhouettes decorate the powder room. BELOW LEFT A nineteenth-century striped "Venetian" carpet runs in front of a Gothic bookcase, now used for linens. BELOW RIGHT The kitchen was designed by architect and homeowner Jim Joseph to take better advantage of the former conservatory.

**ABOVE LEFT** The yellow bedroom includes a mid-nineteenth-century ingrain carpet, American patchwork quilts, and a monumental New York classical armoire on the right. **LEFT** The red bedroom features a "Venetian" carpet and a French Empire bed. **ABOVE** A robust classical New York mahogany bed sits on informal matting that harkens back to materials used in the early nineteenth century.

increased the acreage to approximate the original 1830s plot and have updated and refined the landscape. "We wanted to make a rational path along the property and connect different aspects of the landscape." Several of the outdoor garden rooms initiated by the Van Dykes have now grown to a spectacular scale. A dark blue swimming pool has been perfectly incorporated into a towering hemlock-bordered space. A tennis court was recently added, and an allée of fastigiate beech trees was planted on the west axis to connect the pond.

The couple worked on "one room at a time to find balance between what was meant to be left and not restored at all and what begged rethinking," recalls Joseph. The ability to find harmony is a talent that both men have perfected. At Forth House, the teachings of Euterpe, the Greek muse of music and poetry, and Thalia, the Greek muse of architectural science, are seen in the achievement of symmetry and the play between the refined and the relaxed. Scott and Jim's talents readily evolve and manifest here in this most inspirational environment.

GLENBURN

1836

THE AUTHOR THOMAS WOLFE WROTE of Glenburn, which he renamed "Grandfather Joel's house" in his 1935 novel *Of Time and the River*, "The great rambling old house, which had been so lovely in the moon-enchantment of the night before was no less beautiful by day . . . It sat there in the hollow of the hill, embowered in rich green and shaded by the leafy spread of its green maples." Grandfather Joel was based on Stephen Henry Olin of Glenburn, whom Wolfe met while staying next door at Foxhollow Farm in the 1920s. The central character in Wolfe's book, Joel Pierce, was modeled on Stephen Henry's grandson Olin Dows, a friend of the writer from Harvard who had invited Wolfe to visit Rhinebeck.

In 1830, Thomas Tillotson, surgeon general and later New York's secretary of state, deeded his twelve-year-old granddaughter Julia Lynch sixty-six acres of wooded hemlocks that he owned because "as a child she used to play in the stream and the falls and asked her grandfather to give it to her," wrote her granddaughter and namesake Julia Olin.

Janet and James Lynch, Julia's parents, built Glenburn on this inherited land in 1836 when Julia was eighteen and the family spent summers near the waterfall of the Fallsburg Creek on the property. Glenburn was a name coined from the Scottish "brook in a glen." The original home was an early example of the American Romantic movement in architecture, which diverted from the formality of the Greek Revival. In 1843 Julia married Reverend Stephen Olin and moved to Middletown, Connecticut, where he served as president of Wesleyan University.

Julia Olin moved back to Glenburn after her husband died in 1851 and lived there until her own death in 1879. Her death immediately followed that of her best friend and cousin, Mary Garrettson, who had maintained residence at Wildercliff. The intimate connection between the two families had begun when Julia's grandfather Thomas Tillotson introduced Mary's parents to each other while they were staying at Grasmere. At Glenburn, Julia raised her only son, Stephen Henry, who was the same age as his playmate Henry James, who often stayed nearby at his uncle Augustus James's home Linwood. Henry James describes his time at Rhinebeck in *A Small Boy and Others*, published in 1913.

Continuing her husband's religious teachings, Julia taught Sunday school to a gathering of local children from a stone bench, nestled into a glen of hemlocks near the top of the Fallsburg Creek. Eventually these meetings moved into the Hillside Chapel, which she built in 1855 on the Albany Post Road in Rhinebeck.

Stephen Henry Olin, who had inherited Glenburn upon his mother's death, was left to tend to two daughters, Alice and Julia, when his wife, Elsie Barlow, died after giving birth to her second daughter in 1882. The two girls were then brought up at the imposing townhouse of their maternal grandfather, Samuel L. M. Barlow, at 1 Madison Avenue on Madison Square in Manhattan. When Samuel died, their father moved them to a townhouse at 136 East Nineteenth Street, near Gramercy Park, which was filled to the brim with heavy Victorian furniture covered in suffocating upholstery. In contrast, the girls spent six months of the year at Glenburn with their French governess, Louise, while their father joined them on weekends. Louise taught the sisters French and they in turn conversed in French until they were married.

Alice described their time at Glenburn as idyllic: "A deep cut gives a Raphaelesque view of mountains in the distance with a bit

of river framed by large trees. A brook runs close to the house with a pond edging the back lawn. Two waterfalls, one of considerable size, splash even in the driest of summers. Two miles of paths lead up and down rocky hills covered with moss and fern. It is as romantic a spot

PREVIOUS SPREAD Henry Bacon built Glenburn's massive living room, with its central Palladian window, for Stephen Henry Olin in 1914. The room, which was once a favorite of Franklin Delano Roosevelt, was recently decorated by Carey Maloney of M (Group). Artist Walton Ford created the dramatic elephant on the wall to the right. ABOVE The Colonial Revival design of the house is a result of the work of several noted architects over time including Harrie T. Lindeberg, Henry Bacon, and Theodore W. Dominick.

one can wish for and when I came to it at eight years old I gave it my undying love." The sisters would swim in the natural pool at the top of the falls, play tennis, garden, and ride their ponies.

The contrast to their life in the city, which included lunches with Edith Wharton and artists at The Players club around the corner on Gramercy Park South, made an indelible impression on the girls who both would spend time in Dutchess County when they grew up. Alice wed Tracy Dows in 1903 at Glenburn under the arch of the library entrance, where her grandmother had been married in 1843.

In her autobiography, *From Gaslight to Dawn*, Julie Chanler (as she was then called) sketches a life filled with visits from a young Franklin Delano Roosevelt and car rides with neighbor John Jacob Astor IV down to Poughkeepsie. After one of these rides, Astor

presented her with a gift. Julia exclaimed, "Holy code of prunes and prisms! A man, not of my family, was offering me a present and a tennis racquet at that, when I loathed tennis. Perhaps if it had been something else—but why speculate!"

In the years after the turn of the century, architect Harrie T. Lindeberg began remodeling Glenburn for Stephen Henry Olin. Lindeberg, who was recommended by the painter Charles Dana Gibson, had been trained by Stanford White. He incorporated the fashionable Colonial Revival style into the existing Romantic architectural composition, painting the house a crisp white. Working in Rhinebeck in 1904 was prescient as he was soon conceptualizing the plan for the adjacent Foxhollow Farm for Alice and Tracy Dows. Olmsted Brothers was hired in 1906 to address Glenburn's landscape. Soon after, in 1914, Henry Bacon,

GLENBVRN
MAGNI · PRAEDII · PARS · EXIGVA
A · D · MDCLXXXXVII
AB · ANNA · BRIT · REG
HENRICO  BEEKMAN.
CONCESSVM
INDE · A · D · MDCCXIII
HENRICO · F
TRANSCRIPTVM
INDE · A · REI · PVBL · COND · I · A · AVTEM · DOM · MDCCLXXVI
MARGARETHAE · F
ROBERTI · R · LIVINGSTON · IVDICIS · CLARISS · CONIVGI
LEGATVM
INDE · A · D · MDCCLXXXX
THOMAE · TILLOTSON · GENERO
TRADITVM
A · QVO · A · D · MDCCCXXX
IVLIAE · M · LYNCH · NEPTI
QVAE · POSTEA · V · CL · STEPHANO · OLIN · D · D · NVPSIT
DONO · DATVM
ILLA · MVLTO · ANNOS · EO · SVB · TECTO · BEATE · COMPLEVIT
VSQVE · AD · A · D · MDCCCLXXVIIII

HARVM · V · ANIMARVM
CLARISS · ET · VENERABILISS
EMORIA · AC · VIRTVTES
HAS · AEDES
VSQVE · CCI ANI

OPPOSITE The Latin inscription etched into the glass panes of the living room windows narrates the lineage of Glenburn. **ABOVE AND BELOW** The windows are decorated with the Beekman, Livingston, Tillotson, and Lynch coats of arms, who all once owned the property.

the designer of the Lincoln Memorial in Washington, D.C., was brought on to design the "big room" with its immense Palladian window, which incorporated early nineteenth-century stained- and etched-glass panels with illustrations of the Tillotson, Lynch, Livingston, and Beekman coats of arms.

Shortly after selling Foxhollow Farm, Olin Dows and his mother, Alice, installed themselves in 1937 at Glenburn, where Olin hosted the Dutchess County Historical Society and discussed his family home's history. He noted, with quiet pride, that "this piece of land has not been sold since the time of the first deeds," having passed from one generation of the family to another.

Dows immediately began a restoration project with architect Theodore W. Dominick from Washington, D.C., that included the transformation of the old carriage house into a painting studio and the removal of a superfluous wing. Neighbor Veronique Firkusny fondly remembers that Olin lent the Big Apple Circus his studio, when they were based next door at Southlands (the riding academy established by Deborah Dows in the 1930s) during February, its off season. The sublime height of the ceiling in his studio was ideal for the acrobats and trapeze artists to practice their routines.

The ancestral connection to the site resonated particularly with Olin Dows, whose relationship to the region was the subject of much of his artwork. His murals, which line the walls of the Rhinebeck and Hyde Park post offices, had been exhibited at the Art Students League in New York prior to their installation in 1939, illustrate local folklore and historic sites. He conceived of this project with his good friend and neighbor President Franklin Delano Roosevelt.

The collaboration of the two men, distant cousins through their Beekman lineage, who shared a common interest in local history, produced a pair of post offices that replicated regional Dutch architecture. In the case of the Rhinebeck Post Office, the inspiration was the Kip-Beekman-Livingston House built in 1698 in Rhinecliff. Olin was instrumental in the development of Roosevelt's WPA project, and administered much of the program with his oversight. The vernissage of the installed murals in the post office was attended by heads of state and photographed by Margaret Bourke-White.

A book project, *Franklin Roosevelt at Hyde Park*, which Dows published in 1949, pays homage to his friend and confidant and includes an illustration of the living room at Glenburn. The accompanying text reads: "In June 1942, he [Roosevelt] brought King George II of Greece and Crown Princess Martha of Norway to tea with my mother and a few neighbors she had invited to Glenburn. Our house is an old one, and the small place had never been sold but has descended in the family from the original Beekman grant . . . When the Roosevelt house at Hyde Park was being remodeled in 1915, F.D.R. had the fixtures in our big room copied for his front hall." The book also included an illustration by Dows of Oak Lawn, where Eleanor had been raised by her Livingston grandmother.

Dows eventually married, in 1950, the Chilean Carmen Vial de Senoret Browne, who moved to Glenburn with her son, Luis. Glenburn was left to Luis when Olin died in 1981. Soon after, Luis disposed of his step-father's archive and sold the ancestral property out of the family for the first time.

The present owners engaged Carey Maloney and Hermes Mallea of M (Group) to execute an extensive renovation, which included weaving a contemporary infrastructure within the historic fabric of the property. Updating the interior circulation was challenging because of the idiosyncrasies of the nontraditional irregular floor plan. Color expert Donald Kaufman was summoned to Glenburn to select the palette. And most importantly, the appreciation of the view of the original Olmsted Brothers' magnificent landscape has been reinforced with the strategic placement of several new windows.

---

**ABOVE** A 1903 photograph of the wedding of Tracy Dows and Alice Olin at Glenburn. The charming cottage had diamond-paned windows. **OPPOSITE** The Humpback Bridge, constructed of rough-cut stone in irregular courses, traverses the Fallsburg Creek on the property. Set into an untamed portion of the grounds, it is representative of the Romantic movement in landscape design.

# ROSE HILL

1843

"WHEN YOUR CLIENT IS THE ONE of the most famous colorists in America, you let him pick the paint colors." So declares designer Bill Sofield of his friend and client, the painter Brice Marden. Brice and his wife, Helen, an artist, purchased Rose Hill in Tivoli in 2002 and embarked on an aesthetic inquiry.

A seven-year span of time was needed to complete the renovation of the structure, an 1843 Tuscan-style villa, which was in a compromised condition. The collaboration between the Mardens and Sofield fox-trotted around a celebration of things the couple loves and finding a balance point between keeping the original fabric of the house and introducing new materials. Since Rose Hill was in shambles, the inevitable engineering needed to be negotiated before figuring out where to place beloved objects from travels around the world. The idiosyncratic success of the interiors is the result of this dance and coincidentally echoes the original owner's installation of ethnological artifacts.

General John Watts de Peyster was the builder and probable designer of Rose Hill after marrying Estelle Livingston in 1840. Estelle and John were independently both seventh-generation descendants of Robert, First Lord of Livingston Manor. Estelle and her brother Johnston were born and raised at Green Hill, later known as The Pynes, which was sandwiched among Callendar House, Rose Hill, and the Château de Tivoli. Her inheritance enabled the couple to purchase twenty-five acres in Tivoli in 1843. This land, referred to as Snake Point, was spun off from her cousin

Eugene Livingston's home Eversleigh (later called Teviot), which was directly to the north, creating another link in the chain of connected family seats.

Rose Hill is the third similarly named property belonging to the wealthy de Peyster family, the first of which was located outside Edinburgh in Scotland. The second property, a farm belonging to John's great-grandfather, was located within the area of present-day Kips Bay in Manhattan. This merchant family was among the elite members of early New York society that emigrated from Holland, as Amsterdam had been their interim European address before the French Huguenot family made their way to the New World.

The eccentric General John Watts de Peyster was unanimously considered a holy terror. His reputation deteriorated locally following the estrangement of his wife, Estelle, and their four children. In fact, John had installed on the third floor of Rose Hill's

---

PREVIOUS SPREAD Rose Hill is perched on a steep escarpment overlooking the Hudson River. The tower at the rear of the house is visible on the right. ABOVE Blocks of ice floating down the Hudson in winter are seen from the second floor. OPPOSITE The main entry leads to the porte cochere and beyond to the tower's entrance. FOLLOWING SPREAD *4 (Bone)*, 1987–88, by Brice Marden, hangs above the sofa in the living room, and a painting by Helen Marden has been placed over an eighteenth-century fireplace from Bath, England.

**ABOVE** In another corner of the living room, above a Burmese daybed, is *Letter About Rocks #3 (Blue Ground)*, 2007–10, by Brice Marden. **BELOW** Gaetano Pesce designed the table, which rests on a North Indian rug in the "river room." The floor is Chinese marble.

tower, located toward the back of the house, a Gatling gun aimed at the bistre-gray stone avenue leading up to the house as a deterrent to his first son, Johnston Livingston de Peyster, with whom he had a particularly contentious relationship. At one point, he even chiseled Johnston's name off the plaque that still hangs on Rose Hill's porte cochere.

When Estelle and John finally separated in 1891, he reimbursed Estelle for her contribution of 5,654 dollars toward the purchase of the property while cynically complimenting her obsessive voluntary maintenance of the ivy-covered St. Paul's Episcopal Church in Tivoli. Upon their divorce, Estelle immediately moved across the street to The Pynes, the house her brother Louis had inherited from their father, John Swift Livingston.

In the late eighteenth century, entrepreneur Pierre Delabigarre mapped out a Utopian village in Dutchess County, which he named Tivoli after the early Roman summer retreat that housed Hadrian's Villa. In 1795, Delabigarre built his Château de Tivoli on the property, and lived there with his wife. He had married one of the numerous Margaret Beekmans, whose sister Eliza finally merged the two family names when she wed Peter William Livingston and named her son Horatio Delabigarre Livingston. The Utopian village failed financially and Robert "The Chancellor" Livingston came to the rescue by purchasing a large portion of the village.

Estelle and John's son Johnston, who was named for his Uncle Johnston Livingston, went on to become mayor of Tivoli. With his wife and three daughters, he moved into Delabigarre's Château de Tivoli, which was on the present-day grounds of The Pynes. A second son, Colonel Frederic de Peyster, married Mary Livingston, sister of John Henry Livingston, owner of Clermont. The intention of creating a family compound along the shores of Tivoli was never realized due to disputes among this branch of the de Peyster family.

The grounds of Rose Hill were composed of formal box parterres, first-growth hemlock and pine forests, and a cemetery reserved for parrots and dogs. In his 1909 book, *The History of Dutchess County*, Frank Hasbrouck described the property as "one of the loveliest spots conceivable. It is especially so through the care taken to preserve the primeval trees, of which there were nearly fifty varieties upon the grounds. There are ravines spanned by simple bridges, precipices, a small artificial lakelet, hills, dales, dells, and curious roads climbing rough elevations." The Saugerties Lighthouse and the site of the old Tivoli-Saugerties ferry are visible from the second floor with its magnificent view.

De Peyster added a library to the back of the house in 1860. He self-righteously posted a sign in the room that simply read "Shut Up." The library had been described as a curiosity shop; visitors viewed basalt sculptures of Aztec gods, bronzes, and an array of Damascus and Javanese swords as well as assorted firearms, which some found unsettling for a man often described as confrontational and vindictive. During de Peyster's tenure, the library contained between 20,000 and 30,000 volumes, mostly duplicates of the general's own work, which he published at a furious rate. They

**OPPOSITE** In the sitting room, one of Helen Marden's paintings hangs over an Indian Rainforest marble fireplace. *Untitled*, a 1997–98 photograph by Swiss artists Peter Fischli and David Weiss, is on the wall on the right. The ceiling light comes from Nilufar Gallery in Milan.

ranged from *The History of the Manapiu* and *The Ancient Netherlanders* to history tomes on the wars in which he had participated all signed under the pseudonym "Anchor."

Rose Hill was a stopping point on the Underground Railroad, and de Peyster had held conference with Abraham Lincoln on the subject of slavery. He had written extensively on "The War of the Slaveholders" and "The Oligarchy Against the People" in the 1860s. Two long tunnels originating under the house and continuing to a gully by the Hudson River lend credence that de Peyster was a cog in the Underground Railroad.

The general was deeply involved in the evolution of the village of Tivoli. In 1868, he donated land on Livingston Road, present-day Woods Road, in order to build St. Paul's Episcopal Church. After quarreling with the vicar in 1892, he converted to Methodism and built a Methodist church in a more prominent location around the corner. He financed the John Watts de Peyster Hook and Ladder Company in a brick building across from the new church in 1895, replacing a wooden firehouse erected by his son Johnston. When Johnston became mayor of Tivoli in 1900, the general declared that he was not permitted to attend meetings, which took place in the trustees' room of his firehouse. Family relations were never reconciled, and Rose Hill was deeded to the Leake and Watts Orphan Home in 1905, two years before the general's death.

In 1964, Rose Hill was purchased by Dorothy Day for 78,000 dollars. Day was co-founder of the *Catholic Worker*, the newspaper initiated to express her pacifist philosophy. A farming commune was established on-site and the printing presses for the newspaper were brought up from New York City. Day became an early spokesperson for what she referred to as her nonviolent revolution. Her timing dovetailed with the mounting public resistance to the Vietnam War, but eventually by the mid-1970s, interest dissipated until Ethan Emery, a grandson of artist Charles Dana Gibson, purchased the property from Day. He lived in the schoolhouse on the property in anticipation of an unrealized renovation program for the house.

At the time of his 2006 retrospective at The Metropolitan Museum of Art, current Rose Hill owner Brice Marden commented in a *New York Times* article, "You're really influenced by where you're painting. One of the biggest things is the light. If there was a 'eureka' moment, it was in front of Rothko . . . Rothko was talking about light and spirituality." Marden is not the first painter to be influenced by the area—Thomas Cole, Asher Durand, and Frederic Edwin Church established the Hudson River School in this region.

Marden lets the location dictate his work habits, which often include observing the sun or lack thereof. In discussing a third version of a work started at Rose Hill, he observes that the looping forms "might have come with working by the Hudson." The serpentine land area, Snake Point, the spot on which he paints, has been highly influential in his work. Marden continues, "It's very interesting. This is a very abstract, formal enterprise. And then you turn around and you have the river."

---

Two Moroccan rugs from the Mardens' extensive textile collection lead to the Aga cooker in the kitchen. Japanese fabrics on a red butterfly chair, Berber pots on the top of a hutch, and a Pennsylvania yellow-ware bowl on the table punctuate this colorful space.

**LEFT** In Brice Marden's study, Chinese scholar's rocks have been placed on surfaces around the room, including two Chinese tables. A Moroccan textile covers the daybed. **ABOVE AND BELOW** In the "tower bedroom," a red Turkish Tulu rug covers the bed, while Moroccan rugs have been laid across the floor.

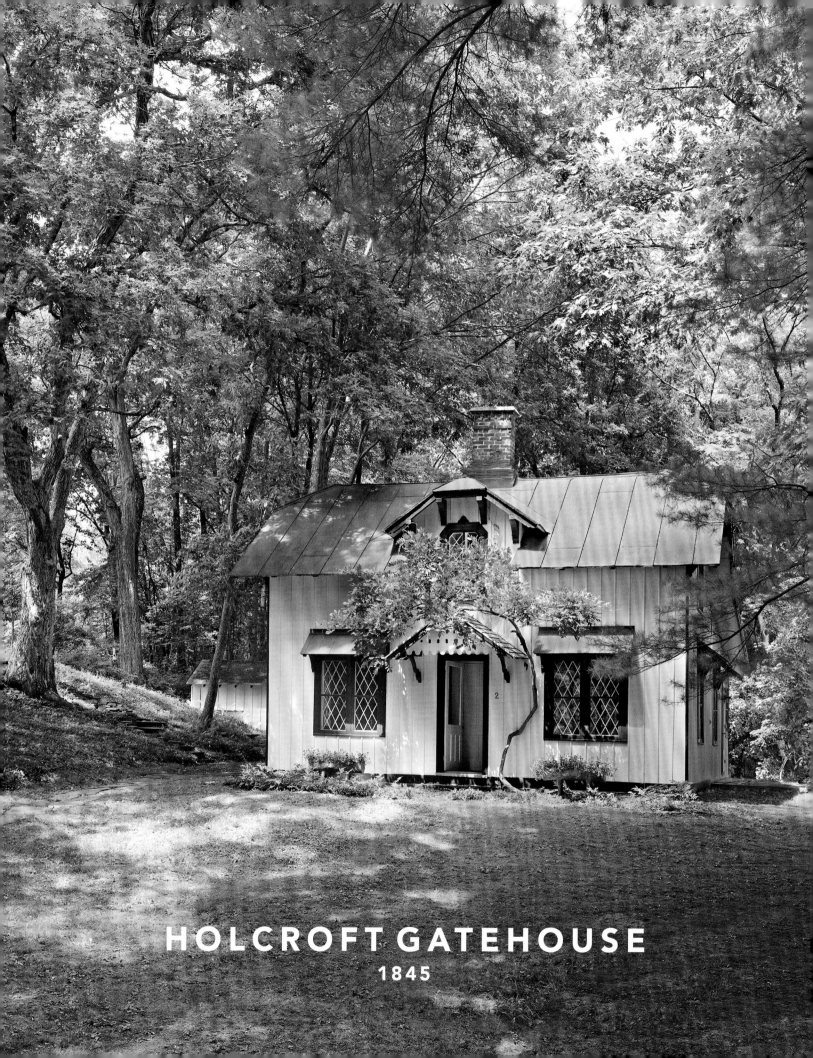

# HOLCROFT GATEHOUSE
## 1845

AN ENCHANTING GATEHOUSE still greets visitors at the entrance to the mile-long driveway that leads to Holcroft, the country seat originally built by Elizabeth Livingston and Edward Hunter Ludlow. The current brick house replaced a Carpenter Gothic home built in the 1840s, which formed a cohesive architectural statement with its gatehouse, now a charming cottage. Nestled cozily between Holcroft and Northwood. Tambra Dillon, executive director of Hudson Hall, has called this home since 2006. The gatehouse had been sold for one dollar during the Depression to the McGregors, who were the caretakers of Holcroft. It was subsequently owned in the 1980s by Adam Horovitz of the Beastie Boys who often strolled down the entrance drive to join Eliot Hawkins, the present owner of Holcroft, for drinks.

Dillon had returned to America after several years in Ireland. She had a "regional epiphany" while a guest at the 2003 opening of DIA:Beacon and immediately started looking for a home in Columbia County once she became the executive director of the Fisher Center for the Performing Arts at Bard College in Annandale-on-Hudson. The scale and informal decoration of the house recalls the original genteel Romanticism of architect A. J. Downing, who was the period's most esteemed commentator on rural taste.

Similarly detailed houses appear in A. J. Downing's 1842 book *Cottage Residences*, which espoused the moralistic philosophy that clean and beautiful houses produce spiritually enlightened people. For him, the appeal of the Picturesque, which was landscaping's answer to the style of this home, was expressed through the controlled wildness still evident as one passes through the gates of Dillon's property.

Entertaining in the summer is alfresco on her tidy adjoining plateau of land to the west, often making good use of the stone cooking pit she installed herself. Winter dinners of up to eight guests are given in the dining room with the nearby fire exiting the center chimney in a characteristically Downing-esque manner reminiscent of the architect's beautifully articulated engravings, diamond-paned windows included. "This is a magical place and a dream come true," says Dillon. "The community on Woods Road is sublime. Except the bears!"

OPPOSITE The board-and-batten Holcroft Gatehouse—a storybook cottage set in the woods   subscribes to the Romantic-style canon.
ABOVE The sitting room was converted from a breezeway in 1957.
RIGHT The living room has original diamond-paned windows and is furnished with mid-century local flea market finds.

# SOUTHWOOD

1849

HART PERRY AND HIS WIFE, DANA, are the present owners of Southwood. In 1967, Hart spotted the house while riding on the bridal path, which connects the string of Livingston properties along Woods Road in Germantown emanating north from Clermont. Having previously rented Grasmere and Sylvania, Hart's parents, Hart, Sr., and Beatrice, known as "Beatie," became tenants at Holcroft. Arriving on horseback through the path, Hart, Jr., came upon Southwood, which at the time was boarded up, having fallen on grim times but appearing as a time capsule. By 1969, Hart's parents, looking to put down more permanent roots, purchased the property on eighty-six acres, which Hart noted, "was complete and unimproved." The outhouse was still intact, as were the outbuildings: a coach house, mill, Gothic gatehouse, and Colonial Revival kennel approaching the grandeur of the equine accommodations at the Château de Chantilly for the former owner's pack of chows.

This property was part of a subdivision of Clermont that occurred in 1845 following the death of New York State Senator and Lieutenant Governor Edward P. Livingston two years earlier. As the husband and cousin of Robert "The Chancellor" Livingston's daughter Elizabeth, who inherited Clermont, Edward had been allowed, following her death in 1829, to continue residing at Clermont. Despite his remarriage to Mary Broome, this alliance proved difficult for Edward's surviving five children to ignore upon his death. Ultimately, 20,000 dollars and a portion of the furnishings of Clermont dispatched Mary to Poughkeepsie so that her stepchildren could more easily hammer out the details relating to their parent's patrimony.

The properties included in Clermont's subdivision eventually were listed on the National Register of Historic Places as the Clermont Estates Historic District in 1979, and were subsumed in 1990 into the Hudson River National Historic Landmark District. The application for registry states that the district is significant because it "consists of a collection of nineteenth-century country estates that cohesively retain, both structurally and environmentally, the original intents of their wealthy, style-conscious builders . . . and which take advantage of the extravagant natural surroundings. The

**PREVIOUS SPREAD** Southwood sits on an elevation overlooking the Hudson River. The 1860 gazebo serves as an observation point. **LEFT** An early panoramic photograph of Southwood illustrates the property's landscaping at the turn of the century. **OPPOSITE** The mirror in the hallway is one of a pair. Its mate hangs at Midwood.

Clermont Estates Historic District is unique in the nation." Although not strictly a planned community, the swath of properties maintain many similarities; among them are endless bucolic meandering driveways, bridle paths along the Hudson, and views of the Catskills, or, as the family historically referred to them, "our mountains."

The portion of the 1845 subdivision on which Southwood stands was deeded to Mary Livingston by her father. With her new husband, Levinus Clarkson, she built the house found on the site today in a transitional Greek Revival–Italianate style. The third story and mansard roof were added in 1880. Levinus died in 1861, leaving two young sons, Edward, born in 1850, and Robert, in 1855. Eventually, Robert moved into neighboring Midwood following his parents further subdivision of the property. Edward stayed with his widowed mother at Southwood until she died in 1898, and then became ostracized from his family and community when he married Rachel Coons, the daughter of the family chef, who lived across from the Southwood Chapel. Despite his being related to every soul on the river within ten miles, the union caused his family members to request that Edward rescind his membership at the Edgewood Club. The couple then moved into another circle of Hudson Valley society, hosting yearly picnics at Southwood for the Coons family and the staffs of every country seat along the Hudson River.

---

The house passed to Edward's niece Amy and her husband, Kellock Myers, then down through the Myers family until the Perrys' ownership in 1969. Hart, Sr., had spoken before Congress on his version of the principles of microeconomics and the prototype of the United States Development and Loan Fund, which granted loans to businesses in developing markets as a solution to stimulate the economy. "Beatie" had been the co-owner of the Gres Gallery in Washington, D.C., which exhibited Fernando Botero, Yayoi Kusama, and Grace Hartigan. An artist in her own right, "Beatie" had her sculpture studio at Southwood and many examples of her work still punctuate the grounds. The couple had a reputation as the best dancers in the Hudson Valley. This was mainly because, according to Hart, "My mom did all the work while they were dancing—all the difficult twirling was due to her talent."

After inheriting the house, Hart and Dana started to spend much more time in Germantown, coming to the conclusion that they could base their respective film careers as well as their shared documentary film company, Perry Films, at Southwood. Dana was the recipient in 2015 of the Academy Award for Best Documentary Short Subject as producer of *Crisis Hotline: Veterans Press 1*. Hart, who was the youngest cameraman working on the 1969 film *Woodstock*, recently completed the film *Willie Mitchell: Solid Soul* in 2017. It traces the origins of soul music and is narrated by Keith Richards and Al Green. While it is often hard to draw direct correlations between the creative process and the environment in which a project develops, Hart offers, "There is something about always knowing that we can look at the magical view, which pushes us on and inspires creativity in our work."

TEVIOT

1850

IN 1843, EUGENE AUGUSTUS LIVINGSTON—a son of Robert L. Livingston and grandson of Robert "The Chancellor" Livingston—managed, after a series of machinations, to trade the dilapidated house at New Clermont, which he had just inherited, for an empty piece of land next door, just to the south, formerly belonging to his younger brother Montgomery. Eugene commented upon inheriting the property that at this point "the home didn't show well," after communicating his disappointment that this was the sole patrimony being left him by his father. The property though had a spectacular view across the Hudson River that included the isthmus leading to Esopus Creek. For his part, Montgomery, who was an artist, was happy to find inspiration in the elegant, if somewhat dog-eared, environment his grandfather The Chancellor had designed at New Clermont.

On this land, in 1850, Eugene built himself a house in the Gothic Revival style that had overtaken the Greek Revival style in popularity. This school of architecture was propelled to the forefront of fashion by architect A. J. Davis. Eugene was able to finance construction not from his inheritance, which was slim, but from the dowry of his wife, Harriet Coleman. The house, humble in scale, was originally called Eversleigh. An example of a cottage orné as described by A. J. Davis, it was ostensibly a farmhouse—but perhaps a farmhouse in the way that Marie Antoinette's Hameau de la Reine at Versailles was a shepherdess's village. The local materials are simple, yet there is a finesse of detail resulting from the attention paid by the original anonymous architect and subsequently reinforced by Sam Trimble, the architect responsible for the present incarnation of the house.

The vocabulary of the original Gothic detail on the south porch is now continued around the house, creating an example of what was considered the most important contribution from A. J. Davis's canon: the transitional space. The earliest demonstration of this was at Blithewood, in Annandale-on-Hudson, now demolished, and at Montgomery Place in Red Hook, downriver a few miles. A. J. Davis explained his desire to form an experiential "connection with

site"—the interrelationship between house and environment that formed the essence of the contemporary Picturesque design philosophy. The porch, or veranda, is such a key component at Teviot that several distinct areas with different purposes are used throughout the seasons. Trimble, inspired by A. J. Davis, continued his nineteenth-century philosophy here.

Teviot was built by a member of the Partiarchs, an extremely select group of twenty-five men handpicked by Ward McAllister, the self-appointed arbiter of New York society of the time. This group gave elaborate parties on the second floor of Delmonico's at Fifth Avenue and 26th Street. Eugene's family eventually included seven children, who were frequently the subjects of such prominent photographers as Mathew Brady and Gustave LeGray.

The property was sold upon Eugene's death to Eugene Schieffelin in 1893 and subsequently to others before being purchased by Howland Davis and his wife, Laura Livingston, in 1923. They renamed the property Teviot, after the river in Scotland where Robert, the First Lord, was born. Howland was mild mannered, the perfect counterpoint to Laura, who was considered fierce and formidable. Her grandson George, who still lives nearby, remembers that when he was a child in the 1940s and 1950s, society was stratified. "There was a very closed proper circle living along the Hudson. We hung out with the kids at the Edgewood Club across Woods Road. We were taught to be very pleasant to the kids in town, but we didn't play with them. It was completely anachronistic by the middle of the twentieth century, but you didn't argue with the matriarchs, and my grandmother always was the one who

---

**PREVIOUS SPREAD** The view from Teviot includes Roundtop Mountain, originally part of landholdings belonging to the Livingston family. **ABOVE** The grass from the fields surrounding the house is cut and baled in the fall. **OPPOSITE** Members of Eugene Livingston's family were often photographed during the nineteenth century.

set the tone." He continues, "This was a society which was totally blind to what was going on in the world . . . waspish to the extreme, with no emotions, but lots of joking to let off the emotional steam."

Howland was the chairman of the Taconic State Parks Commission, which in 1962 had purchased Clermont, Teviot's immediate neighbor to the north, from Alice Delafield Clarkson Livingston, with whom he had several misunderstandings. Following the sale, Howland undiplomatically referred to Clermont as "my house," even to Alice's daughter Honoria, who continued living at Sylvan Cottage on a small parcel of the property that she owned. He delayed Clermont from opening as a museum for several years after Alice Delafield Livingston passed away in 1964.

Howland and Laura's son Howland, nicknamed "Bunk," married Frances, known as "Fuzz," and in the 1950s moved from the barn, which offered little privacy, to Teviot's main house. They raised their four children in this bucolic setting. The oldest, named Howland as well, was called "Buzz" in an odd conflation of his parents' names. The children played hockey on the cold spring-fed pond that froze over in the winter, and swam there in summer.

In 1964, Bunk's daughter Dennie, looking out from the original porch, had an amusing and unexpected sighting—gliding down the Hudson River in front of Teviot was a life-size dinosaur en route to its home at the World's Fair in New York City. In 2006, the Davises sold Teviot, which encompassed around 100 acres, to *Rolling Stone* founder Jann Wenner and his partner, Matt Nye. The two men hired architect and designer Sam Trimble, with whom they had previously collaborated on several properties, to spruce up the house and grounds. It was then that the Gothic Revival porch was extended around the house to take advantage of the panoramic views.

Further improvements on the property included the construction of a modern pool house in 2012, with a spring-fed pool, and the opening of the viewshed, which, along with the house, had become completely overgrown. "There was not the most positive vibe," Trimble reports. "The place was semi-abandoned with vines choking the house." With its successful revival, perhaps now Jann and Matt's children will be able to spot other errant extinct beasts making their way down the river.

**OPPOSITE** The Gothic Revival moldings in the house were carefully repaired during the recent restoration. The colorful Moroccan rug is part of a large collection **ABOVE** The sculpture in the corner of the living room is by Dustin Yellin. A drawing by Fernando Botero hangs above a French limestone mantel. The red Danish chair is by Nanna Ditzel, and the sofa is by Vladimir Kagan.

**ABOVE** A pair of Frits Henningsen chairs is placed in the corner of the dining room. **OPPOSITE** *St. George and the Dragon*, a fifteenth-century Spanish oil-on-panel hangs next to assorted musical equipment and guitars in the dining room. **FOLLOWING SPREAD** The porch is used most of the year as an extension of the living room.

The pool house was designed by architect Sam Trimble in 2012 using Douglas fir on the walls and black cleft slate for the heated floors. Above the fireplace is a bronze sculpture by Francisco Zúñiga. The 1947 handcrafted oak and rush chairs directly in front of the pool house fireplace are by Charlotte Perriand, from a hotel in Meribel-les-Allues, France.

**ABOVE** The trellis shades all four sides of the pool house.
**BELOW** Benches made with reclaimed stone from a Hudson courthouse line the changing room in the pool house.

# STEEN VALETJE

1851

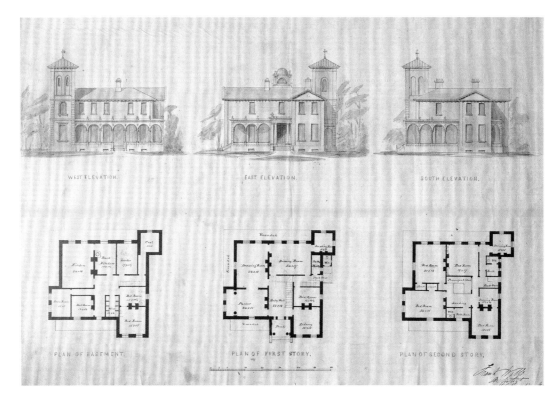

WEST ELEVATION.   EAST ELEVATION.   SOUTH ELEVATION.

PLAN OF BASEMENT.   PLAN OF FIRST STORY.   PLAN OF SECOND STORY.

WHEN LAURA ASTOR MARRIED Franklin Hughes Delano in 1844, her father William Backhouse Astor, Sr., in a none too thinly veiled effort to keep her nearby, gave them the southernmost 100 acres in Red Hook belonging to Rokeby. The name the Delanos gave their new home was inspired by an area on a local 1713 map. "Steen Valetje" translates from the Dutch as "little stony glen," in reference to the rocky brook that ran through the property, which also has been called Mandara and Atalanta.

Known as the most handsome man of his day, Franklin was consul for Chile until the completion of Steen Valetje in 1851. He was involved with his brothers in the shipping concern Grinell, Minturn, and Company. Franklin Delano Roosevelt was to become their great-nephew and reside downriver in Hyde Park.

Laura had grown up next door at Rokeby as the granddaughter of the wealthiest man in the country, John Jacob Astor. Their New York City residence was 45 LaGrange Terrace, now called Colonnade Row. This impressive collection of private dwellings was designed by A. J. Davis in an effort to replicate British row enclaves of the 1830s. Laura's grandfather John Jacob Astor lived in the same terraced row, at number 37.

British architect Frank Wills designed Steen Valetje, as well as many of the furnishings, and created a cohesive expression of the popular Italianate style. Replacing the symmetry and mathematical discipline that had influenced architecture in America throughout the 1830s and 1840s were pastoral references to the Italian countryside that included rambling asymmetrical gestures, belvederes, and the Roman arch. Architect John H. Sturgis contributed the master plan for the interiors in the 1870s when Steen Valetje was perhaps the grandest residential example of the Tuscan style.

In 1878 an Italianate gatehouse was constructed in robust masonry following designs by William Schickel. An immense parlor was added to the south elevation by architect Thomas Stent, who had assisted Alexander Saeltzer with the design of the Astor Library on Lafayette Place, just south of Astor Place. The building now houses Joseph Papp's The Public Theater across from Colonnade Row. The library eventually merged with the Tilden Trust and Lenox Library to become the New York Public Library on Fifth Avenue at Forty-second Street.

Laura and Franklin employed landscape gardener Hans Jacob Ehlers and his son, Louis Augustus, to develop the plans for the grounds. They were familiar with Ehlers's work at Rokeby and Ferncliff, and impressed with his ability to carve poetic swaths throughout the grounds at Rokeby.

By the time the house was enlarged, the couple was spending most of the year in Geneva and Monte Carlo, where Franklin eventually died in 1893. During their travels, Laura noticed a striking glass canopy covering the entrance at the Hôtel Beau Rivage on Lake Geneva, and then ceremoniously offered a sum for it. She had it shipped back to Red Hook, where it remained in place until the neo-Georgian reconfiguration of the house in 1973. Laura passed away in 1902 and left her investments to her eight Chanler nieces and nephews who had grown up at Rokeby.

As they were childless, Laura and Franklin left Steen Valetje to his nephew Warren Delano III and his wife Jenny Walters in 1894. An avid horseman, he lived there until 1920 when his horse became spooked by the sounds of an oncoming train at the Barrytown Station, and he was killed when the horse ran onto the tracks.

PREVIOUS SPREAD Steen Valetje was given a Georgian facade in the 1970s. The 1874 north wing addition was designed by Boston architects John Hubbard Sturgis and Charles Brigham. OPPOSITE A bay window extends off the south parlor, designed by Thomas Stent. ABOVE The original plans by Frank Wills for Franklin Hughes Delano and his wife, Laura Astor, illustrate an American interpretation of a Tuscan-style villa.

**OPPOSITE** The entrance foyer has the original Minton encaustic tiles. **ABOVE** The date of the construction, 1851, is carved into the library mantel. Benjamin Franklin is one of four American Founding Fathers whose portraits were painted on the ceiling of the library.

One of Warren and Jenny's eight children, Laura Franklin Delano, was nicknamed "Polly" after the Apollinaris water she drank exclusively. Laura cut a dashing figure; she eccentrically expressed herself with an artificially accented widow's peak, violet hair, and an overabundant display of jewelry. Laura and Margaret Suckley became the bookend cousin-confidantes of Franklin Delano Roosevelt and were with him when he died in Warm Springs, Georgia.

Laura was the inspiration for the character of Madge Telfair in Thomas Wolfe's novel *Of Time and the River*. Wolfe had met Laura when, as a guest of Olin Dows at Foxhollow Farm, he had been invited to Ferncliff on Independence Day in 1927. She was depicted by Olin Dows in his Rhinebeck Post Office murals in a scene selling food and clothing at the Exchange for Women's Work Thrift Shop. Her brother Lyman, with whom she did not get along, inherited their childhood home, and in 1929 she built her own home, Evergreen Lands, in Rhinebeck, designed by John

Russell Pope. Sara Roosevelt, Franklin's mother, confronted her as the first of the clan to wear red nail polish, exclaiming, "Polly, dear, have you been disemboweling a rabbit?" Lyman and his wife, Leila, were stewards of the house until 1966 when it was sold out of the family.

In July 1949, Eleanor Roosevelt wrote of her visit to Steen Valetje in her famous "My Day" column. Even without the benefit of hearing her highly articulated pronunciation, her point is a strong one. "Driving home we followed as many of the old and

---

**ABOVE** A series of gallery rooms leads from the entrance to the south parlor. **OPPOSITE** In 1878, Italian artisans painted the house's ceilings in the neo-Pompeian style. The grand stairway is illuminated by a skylight. The second-floor bedrooms have transoms that open to allow air to circulate in the summer heat.

unfrequented roads as I could remember, going past Bard College and the old Chanler place and going to see Mrs. Lyman Delano. I could not help thinking that in many ways her old house at Steen Valetje, in spite of being built in the Victorian era, has more charm and sense of being a house where people have lived and really understood and loved their possessions than some houses where you have a feeling that a perfectly impersonal decorator was called in to hang the curtains and lay the rugs and choose and place the furniture . . . That kind of house never gives me a sense of being really representative of the personality of the people who live in it and without some feeling left by various generations a house remains a shell and never becomes a home."

The current 17,000-square-foot house is surrounded by ancient oaks, rolling lawns, a greenhouse, barns, four guesthouses, ponds, and equestrian facilities, along with the chaste Doric pool house.

OPPOSITE The chaste Doric pool house faces the Kingston-Rhinecliff Bridge. ABOVE Many of the country seats dotting the Hudson River commissioned and raced magnificent iceboats in the nineteenth century; some of these are still in use and continue a unique winter tradition. RIGHT The 1878 drawing of Steen Valetje's Italianate gatehouse is by William Schickel.

# WILDERSTEIN

## 1852

IN 1852, THOMAS HOLY SUCKLEY, a descendant of Gilbert Livingston, built an Italianate villa on thirty-two acres of sheep pasture in Rhinebeck purchased from his cousin Mary Garretson, owner of Wildercliff. He hired architect John Warren Ritch to design his home, which he named The Cedars. The means through which he was able to finance his home came from his father, George, the founder of the Greenwich Savings Bank.

His son, Robert Suckley, married Elizabeth Phillips Montgomery in 1884, a relation through Lynch and Livingston cousins. The couple inherited the home in 1888 and immediately embarked on an improvement project with Poughkeepsie architect Arnout Cannon that obscured the previous modest villa.

The mock Teutonic appellation chosen by Robert Suckley for his home refers to an Indian petroglyph on the property. Carved into a large stone that is partially immersed in the Hudson River is the image of a Native American. The name Wilderstein is a derivation of wilde for "savage," and stein for "stone." This pictograph, which had originally been thought to memorialize the transfer of property from the Native Americans to the Dutch in 1688, is now partially submerged in the Hudson River.

The eccentric composition of the house, built with the irregular massing of the Queen Anne style, included a wraparound veranda, a five-story tower, a windmill, and a plethora of elaborate decorative

embellishments. The intentional asymmetry is dotted with graphic sunbursts and fish-scale shingles and culminates at its apex with a conical roof that accentuates the dominant vertical line of the tower. The original polychrome colors have recently been reintroduced after more than 100 years. Mauve, Tuscan tan, and green now give an accurate impression of how the house must have appeared upon completion in 1888.

Robert was in constant communication with Cannon; they implemented many of the Victorian period's technological advances, which included a burglar alarm and a dumbwaiter. He became heavily invested in the development of electricity, and was an eager competitor of Thomas Edison. His new technology allowed electricity to be installed in the house through the hydroelectric generator

PREVIOUS SPREAD The Queen Anne Wilderstein house has an impressive five-story tower. The 1888 veranda on the southwest side was originally fitted with removable glass panels. The windows on the second floor and the extended chimneys are original to the 1852 home. ABOVE Margaret Suckley completed the Suckley-Montgomery genealogical chart. OPPOSITE The Stick-style veranda frames the view of the landscape created by Calvert Vaux and beyond to the Hudson River.

Robert placed nearby on the Landsman Kill. Upon completion the family employed ten domestic servants and twelve men to work on the grounds and farm. The carriage house with its spectacular onion dome, which was also designed by Cannon, now awaits restoration.

Joseph Burr Tiffany, a younger cousin of Louis Comfort Tiffany, designed five of the principal living spaces on the first floor in 1888. His meteoric ascent as an interior designer began after working as a clerk at his uncle's store at 15 Union Square. He had studied dec-

OPPOSITE Joseph Burr Tiffany used quarter-sawn oak for the Jacobean-style entrance hall, which has tooled leather walls. ABOVE The stair hall features grasscloth walls from 1907 with a band of 1888 William Morris pomegranate wallpaper and stained-glass windows designed by Joseph Burr Tiffany. FOLLOWING SPREAD The library's stenciled ceiling was recently restored. The Berlin torchères and chandelier are part of the Flemish Gothic–style design.

orative arts under Adrian Pottier, nephew of the owner of Pottier and Stymus, then the leading decorators in Manhattan. The white and gold room at Wilderstein, conceived in the Louis XVI style, was a collaboration between Tiffany and Pottier and Stymus. The Aubusson carpet, which was specifically woven for this room to accommodate every corner and piece of molding, now lies in a delicate and worn state, wrapped in paper in the attic. The last time it was rolled out was under the supervision of Wilderstein's Executive Director Elise Barry with Teviotdale's Victor Cornelius and Richard Barker in the 1980s. The circular canvas set into the ceiling above the silk covered walls of this room was painted on-site by Henry Siddons Mowbray in 1889.

Tiffany designed the dining room with stained-and-etched-glass representations of the Livingston, Tillotson, Lynch, and Chew armorial crests. Margaret Suckley told her young friend Ray Armater that "My mother was very hospitable—she loved having the house completely full. Sometimes we had twenty cousins staying here."

Tiffany also designed the oak entrance hall that was covered in tooled leather and sported the Montgomery griffin crowning the newel post. The Flemish Gothic library with its newly restored stenciled ceiling and Berlin iron chandelier and torchères made an impressive waiting area for guests. The Colonial Revival cherry-trimmed parlor was fitted with silver-plated light fixtures and hardware. Every surface reflects the dark, rich, heavy aesthetic of the late nineteenth century. Tiffany ended his career as head of the Steinway & Sons' art piano department, designing fantastic creations that just happened to have eighty-eight keys.

Calvert Vaux, the landscape designer who, with Frederick Law Olmsted, designed Central Park's master plan in 1857, was brought by Robert Suckley in 1891 to create pleasure grounds. He was assisted by his son Downing Vaux, named for Calvert's mentor and earlier partner, A. J. Downing. The design of the Lodge, or Gatehouse, is credited to Downing Vaux; today it houses the offices of Gregory Sokaris, executive director of Wilderstein Historic Site.

In 1983, Ray Armater, then age twenty-six and the founding member and curator of the Hudson River Maritime Museum in Kingston, met Margaret Suckley, the last family member to reside at Wilderstein. She had sent the museum a note offering the donation of several artifacts from the family's iceboats. Ray was unfamiliar with her name and was unprepared for this fascinating introduction. She invited Ray to tea on the porch at Wilderstein after transporting the iceboat parts to Kingston, and told him about the grandfather clock in the entrance hall that John Jacob Astor IV had rescued in 1909 from the burning Kip-Beekman-Livingston House in Rhinecliff. Ray began stopping by often on his way to work at IBM to oversee the stabilization of the carriage house. Their relationship evolved to include constant visits with plates of chocolate-chip cookies served, while Margaret recounted the seemingly endless and extraordinary experiences throughout her life. Soon Ray succeeded Wint Aldrich as president of Wilderstein Preservation whose board managed to complete the transfer of the historic property into the public sector after the death of Margaret Suckley. "Even with the huge generation gap, we just clicked," recalls Armater. She eventually offered him the opportunity to move into the house, which seemed to serve both parties quite well.

Margaret, sometimes called "Daisy" by close friends, was the granddaughter of the original owner of the property. She was born in the house in 1891 and died there in her 100th year. Margaret was descended from Robert, First Lord of Livingston Manor, through his son Gilbert and from Henry Beekman through her mother, Elizabeth. After her mother died in 1953, Margaret lived in the house with her two bachelor brothers, Arthur and Robert, who were known as the "upstairs-downstairs" Suckleys. The brothers were quietly estranged and were not on speaking terms. Robert, called "Robin," moved to his father's former bedroom on the second floor, while

**LEFT** The hardware in the cherrywood trimmed Colonial Revival parlor was silver-plated to contrast with the damask-upholstered walls. A portrait of Robert Suckley by Casilear Cole hangs over the piano. **FOLLOWING SPREAD** Pottier & Stymus decorated the Louis XVI white and gold room. The 1888 silk wall upholstery remains. Henry Siddons Mowbray painted the cherubic celebration overhead. The mantel is made of onyx and gilt bronze.

Margaret and Arthur occupied the third floor. In the late 1970s, Margaret moved to the first floor where she lived the remainder of her life. Arthur claimed that his vision improved with age due to the fact that he often read upside down. This he would explain in a convincing manner, saying, "Of course people will stare at you on the subway and buses, but you must do it anyway." He was known as a dandy and, among other things, the inventor of the tennis backboard.

Robert would direct dinner guests to the dining room while he remained in the adjacent room, eating from a tray and listening to the conversation next door. Quite aware of this, the guests would strive to reach heights of either intellectual brilliance or wittiness to impress him. Throughout all of her brothers' flamboyant eccentricities, Margaret remained a calming force.

Margaret was related to Eleanor Roosevelt through her Livingston connection and to Franklin Delano Roosevelt through the Beekman family line. When Franklin came back to Hyde Park following his polio diagnosis, Margaret was living in New York City, caring for her aunt Sophia Langdon to secure income in her waning financial circumstances. Margaret soon reconnected with Franklin in Dutchess County, and became his close confidante.

A great deal of Margaret's identity became intertwined with her sixth cousin to whom she was utterly devoted. She was the photo archivist in charge of Franklin's favorite section, local history, at the Franklin D. Roosevelt Presidential Library in Hyde Park for twenty-five years. Margaret gave him Fala, then the country's most photographed and beloved presidential dog, and she was with him in Warm Springs, Georgia, when he died in 1945. After Margaret passed away in 1991, Ray Armater discovered that she had kept Franklin's letters to her in a worn black suitcase behind the door in her childhood bedroom, most addressed to "MM" for "My Margaret." Their relationship was

**ABOVE AND OPPOSITE** The pantry contains many technological innovations from 1888, including the annunciator panel above the speaking tube. The first telephone number for this house was 18, then 4818, and finally the full ten-digit number that persisted in ending with 18. **FOLLOWING SPREAD** The suitcase full of Margaret's letters to and from Franklin Delano Roosevelt was discovered behind the door of Margaret's bedroom.

ABOVE The petroglyph, believed to be Chief Ankony wearing the feathered headdress of an Esopus sachem, memorializes the transfer of property from the Native Americans to the Dutch in 1688. RIGHT A view from the fifth floor of the tower past the Calvert Vaux–designed grounds and Suckley Cove.

documented in Geoffrey Ward's 1995 book, *Closest Companion*. The contents of the house offer a rare and intact repository of one family's household records. The Suckleys saved everything: landscape plans, architects' drawings, textiles, and a voluminous archive of photographs. Margaret noted in 1983, "It's been a family trait, I guess, never throwing anything out. We are all pack rats around here. We never had many servants, we always did for ourselves . . . My mother had a cook, a laundress, and a chamber-maid." There is a telling arc that unfolds through the examination of the names associated with the original architectural plans, interior design, and contents of the house and grounds. Robert did not work while he was designing Wilderstein and listed his occupation as "gentleman" on the census of 1883. Following the financial crisis of 1893 and the family's reversal of fortune, he took the family to the town of Château d'Oex in Switzerland to live at the Pension Château Rosa. He did this for the same reasons that his cousin John Henry Livingston of Clermont took his family to Fiesole, Italy—they were able to conserve assets while continuing to live on a comfortable scale.

Margaret outlived her siblings and resided in the house at Wilderstein until she died in 1991 at ninety-nine and a-half years old—a near centenarian whose experience had been a bridge between two centuries, countless family members, and the vicissitudes of home stewardship.

# EDGEWATER GATEHOUSE
## 1854

EVERY TWENTY YEARS, THE GHOST of architect A. J. Davis seems to appear at the Tuscan-style gatehouse he designed as part of his master plan for Robert Donaldson at Edgewater in Barrytown. Present owner Christine Gummere, grew up in this house. Across the street, its mate, a second gatehouse, reflects his Bracketed Oriental style. Christine's grandfather purchased the two houses for her parents in the 1940s when her father, Richard, arrived at Bard College to serve as the director of admissions. Her mother, Margaret, was a violist and passed her talent and predisposition down to her daughter, a cellist specializing in Baroque music.

In 1976, Christine saw a ghost. When she broached the subject, her mother asked enough questions to indicate that she had seen the same apparition in the 1950s. One of the questions posed had been "Was he wearing a top hat and frock coat?" She described his features and manner in such detail, it was apparent they had seen the same vision. Later, Christine learned that a Bard professor, a previous occupant, had seen something to make him run out and never return. After hearing this tale, she researched A. J. Davis and found an image of the man she had seen.

Davis conceived of the pendant gatehouses while working on the Octagon Library at Edgewater for Robert Donaldson. The two had collaborated at Blithewood, Donaldson's previous home where an 1841 gatehouse still stands.

The two gatehouses were purchased from Chanler Chapman, known as "the most eccentric man in America." Superlatives abound when referring to Chapman, who had grown up at Sylvania, his home previously divided off from Edgewater's property. Speaking at Chanler's memorial ceremony many years later, Christine's father referred to him as "a storm of a man." The novelist Saul Bellow had modeled the erratic character of Eugene in *Henderson the Rain King*, which Bellow wrote while teaching at Bard, on Chanler, whose infamous line to new guests was, "Step in and enjoy the turmoil." His neighbor at Edgewater, Gore Vidal, characterized Chanler in his autobiography, *Palimpsest*, as "a large booming creature with an eerie and unjustified self-assurance."

Chanler's father, renowned essayist John Jay Chapman, had voluntarily burned his arm down to a stump in an act of contrition in 1887 after he had incorrectly accused, then violently assaulted, Percival Lowell, a fellow Harvard student, of flirting with his future wife, Minna Timmons. Chanler's second wife, Elizabeth Chanler Chapman, was one of the "Astor orphans" from Rokeby, and is the subject of John Singer Sargent's magnificent 1893 portrait that hangs in the Smithsonian American Art Museum. According to Sargent, Elizabeth had "the face of the Madonna and the eyes of the child." The couple hired architect Charles A. Platt to design Sylvania in 1905 while living at Edgewater down the hill.

Chanler Chapman ran the *Barrytown Explorer* from 1957 until 1982. He published out of Good Hap, the home his mother commissioned from John Churchill on Sylvania's property in 1933 as a dower house. When his first wife, Olivia James, started divorce proceedings the week he published an article titled "Wives Conk Husbands, Get Sympathy," Chanler purchased the gatehouse so she could move down the hill with their children. The expansive view from the back still looks out on Sylvania's farm. The house sits on Station Hill Road, a quiet dead-end street that delivers a charming miniature white temple at its terminus that once served as the Barrytown Post Office and penny candy store. Today, many Bard College professors and artists call this road home, although there have been no recent paranormal sightings of nineteenth-century phantom architects.

**OPPOSITE** A. J. Davis designed the octagonal gatehouse as part of an unmatched pair for Robert Donaldson. **ABOVE RIGHT** Christine Gummere's cellos are kept in one of the cozy rooms on the first floor. **RIGHT** A bedroom looks out onto Sylvania's expansive fields.

AN INOPPORTUNE MEETING between Rex McVitty and one of the Carmelite nuns inhabiting Ridgely happened one day in 1965. Rex and his wife, Honoria, were living in Sylvan Cottage at Clermont, which was adjacent to the nuns' residence. One afternoon, Rex, who was fond of gardening shirtless, was out collecting wild strawberries. He confessed to Squeaky Hatch in his Scottish brogue, "I flushed a wee nun out of the bushes today." Evidently as he stood up to rest, a startled nun flew out of the bushes and darted away. Rex lurched after her, shouting, "'Oh, Miss Nun, I mean you no harm. Don't run away.'" It was rare for the cloistered nuns, known as The Little Flower Novitiates,who resided at Ridgely since 1946, to interact with the other residents of Woods Road in Germantown.

The house, which later became known as Ridgely, was built in 1855 on the eighty-six acre site of Chancellor Robert Livingston's apple orchard by Elizabeth Clarkson and her husband, artist and gentleman of leisure, George Gibbs Barnwell.

The property was purchased by William Hunt in 1863. He named the house Ridgely after his wife, Elizabeth Ridgely Hunt, who had been born at Clermont in 1825 when it was owned by her grandparents Margaret Maria and Robert L. Livingston. In 1864, the Hunts arrived at the Tivoli train depot with seven children—one with the first name Livingston—and traveled the two miles from there by ferry to Clermont, continuing on to Ridgely by carriage.

Sadly, within three months, Elizabeth died. The children grew up roaming and playing on the grounds that were composed of well-maintained sweeps of lawn punctuated with arrangements of trees, mostly oak, hemlock, ash, elm, and maple. The serpentine paths and drives were laid out with a fluidity characteristic of the nineteenth century. The house was covered with white stucco and had large bay windows that were thought to be designed by A. J. Davis. William's son Thomas Streatfeild Hunt wrote of his father that he flattered himself with a pretense of farming and gardening but passed most of his time in country sports, which included racing with his wife's cousins on horseback along the paths that connected the enfilade of riverfront properties lining Woods Road.

Days were spent at the stables, driving by carriage to the station at Tivoli to collect the mail, swimming in the Hudson, and reading Dickens in the study. Dinner was formally served at five o'clock in the evening and marked with the pronouncement by William Hunt, positioned at the head of the table, "Those that beg shan't have any, and those who don't ask, don't want any." These daily rituals, lasting from 1864 to 1877, established deep family relationships.

By 1889, William Hunt became unable to bear the expense of maintaining Ridgely so it was sold to his son, Thomas, a direct descendant of Robert of Clermont, who had spent his bucolic childhood there. In 1906, a facelift was orchestrated by William Hunt with the hiring of the architectural firm of Austin Lord and James Hewlett to add dining and library wings as well as to move the principal entrance from the river side to the Woods Road access. Today, the Carmelite Sisters meticulously tend to the property, and enjoy the wild strawberries on their side of the bushes.

The east elevation of Ridgely is approached by the original serpentine carriage drive that leads from Woods Road.

# RIDGELY

## 1855

THE POINT

1855

NESTLED DISCREETLY BETWEEN Norrie State and Mills Memorial State Parks in Staatsburg, The Point, despite the disappearance of the trumpet vine and wisteria that once climbed the veranda, still offers an initial poetic Gothic impression. Often described as riddled with decay and deterioration, the villa is presently undergoing the first steps of restoration.

The Point was one of the most important villas in America completed by Calvert Vaux who, along with Frederick Law Olmsted, designed Central Park. Vaux also worked on the adjacent Metropolitan Museum of Art as well as the American Museum of Natural History. The architect was so pleased with the design for the Hoyts, the owners of The Point, that he included it as "Design No. 31. Picturesque Stone Country House," in his 1857 *Villas and Cottages*, giving it the most extensive description in the book.

Built in 1855 for 13,200 dollars with locally quarried bluestone, The Point, so named for the slim peninsula on which it is sited, was the summer home of Lydig Monson and Geraldine Livingston Hoyt, whose family lived there until 1963.

Geraldine Livingston grew up next door at Staatsburgh House with her parents, Maturin and Margaret Livingston, both descendants of Robert Livingston, First Lord of Livingston Manor. Lydig and Geraldine married in 1842 and lived at Staatsburgh House with her parents until 1855 when they began dividing their time between a townhouse at 111 West Fourteenth Street in New York City and their new home designed by Vaux.

The land for The Point was assembled by Lydig, who combined acreage given to his wife by her mother with several purchased contiguous farms. It was not until Geraldine's fifth child was born in 1855 that the couple had cobbled together enough property, total-

ing eighty-seven acres, to be able to hire one of the most prominent architects of the day to design the home and extensive grounds that would reflect their aesthetic and social status.

In 1850, A. J. Downing met Calvert Vaux, while he was in England searching for a complimentary partner to join his practice. Downing and Vaux, as the firm was called, practiced in America until A. J. Downing's premature death in 1852. While on a boat ride down the Hudson, the ship caught fire from overheated engines and Downing drowned trying to save fellow passengers. Vaux soon formed a new partnership with Frederick Withers; Vaux and Withers is the signature on many of the early drawings of The Point. It is during the construction of the Hoyts' house that Vaux, with Olmsted, won the competition for Central Park.

According to A. J. Downing in his 1850 book, *The Architecture of Country Houses*, "What we mean by a villa in the United States is a country house of a person of competence or wealth sufficient to build and maintain it with some taste and elegance . . . a house of larger accommodation, requiring the care of at least three or more servants." The mid-nineteenth century was marked by the use of a vast array of color and texture previously unheard of in America. Vaux, an architect trained in England during the early Victorian period, influenced the evolution of American architecture with this inspired project.

At The Point, Vaux presented a compendium of Picturesque and Romantic details, including many borrowed from the Gothic period in Europe. The Hoyts' home featured quatrefoils and verge boards for the gables, a synthesis of disparate elements from previous decades all melded into a successful nineteenth-century composition.

Juxtaposed with these elements were many bold and unconventional effects using a varied palette and textures. The contrast between the cool weathered bluestone and the reddish brownstone with the different finishes and textures of the roof slates, all married with a dark red pointing mortar, created polychrome stripes.

Many of the inventions at The Point were forerunners to Le Corbusier's "machine for living" of the next century: running water, heat, cooling, and air circulation were manipulated through multiple modern devices. Vaux also introduced hoods and awnings

above the windows and verandas to block or allow the sun to enter. These components were borrowed from British Regency buildings of the early nineteenth century. For The Point, they were made of sheet metal and painted in stripes to approximate canvas awnings.

"A well-balanced irregularity" was Vaux's goal in the design process that is illustrated throughout the exterior of the house. A formal set of massive symmetrical gables greets the visitor and draws the eye to an animated roof line, punctuated by bands of colored slate. In contrast to the former more academic architectural style, Greek Revival, the overall spirit of The Point is one of whimsy.

Proceeding north on the Hudson in 1869, Vaux worked for two years with landscape painter Frederic Edwin Church on the design for his home, Olana. Here, he featured many of the philosophical and intellectual conceits found at the Hoyts' home, paired with a fantastical Persian design vocabulary. Vaux later went on to redesign the landscape at Wilderstein.

Ownership of the house passed to Geraldine and four surviving children upon Lydig's death in 1868. When Geraldine died in 1897 the estate was given to her son Gerald and his wife, Mary, who transformed the interiors of the house to fit with turn-of-the-century tastes. By this time, the charming style that was the core of Vaux's principles of design had fallen out of fashion and was replaced by a return to a more formal symmetry with classical references.

The transformation of the first-floor interiors was at this time undertaken by Robert Palmer Huntington, a consulting partner at the architecture firm Hoppin and Koen. The founding partners, Fran-cis Hoppin and Terence A. Koen, were alumni of McKim, Mead & White, which was concurrently working to enlarge the neighboring Staatsburgh House for Ruth Livingston and Ogden Mills.

Robert Huntington grew up summering in Rhinebeck at Bois Doré. He married Helen Gray Dinsmore in 1892 at The Locusts, her family's home near The Point in Staatsburg. Working briefly in finance for J. Pierpont Morgan, he capriciously switched careers to that of gentleman architect in 1896. In 1910, he and his wife moved into Hopeland House, the Tudor Revival home he had designed for his family. Here his daughter, Helen, was courted by Vincent Astor, whom she married in 1914 before moving into Ferncliff.

While the Vaux-designed interiors on the first floor of The Point are obscured by Huntington's renovation, the second floor maintains original details, such as the simple but robust molding of the mid-nineteenth century, which hugs the tops of the doors and windows. Rarely seen is such a juxtaposition of incompatible styles. The plethora of swags, pilasters, floral bouquets, and broken pediments introduced by Huntington were exactly what Vaux had been militantly working to eradicate.

Lydig, Jr., inherited the property in 1927 and lived there until 1959. He had served as private secretary to Whitelaw Reid, Ambassador to the Court of St. James's in London. Upon the death of Lydig, Jr., his wife, Helen, resided there alone until 1963 when, despite her protestations, she was pressed to accept 300,000 dollars authorized under the Park and Recreation Acquisition Bond Act of 1960 as an alternative to condemning the property.

Robert Moses wanted the property to be able to create a string of acreage connecting Mills Memorial and Norrie State Parks, both of which the state had previously acquired—the location of the Hoyts' home was impeding his goal. The year 1963 was apocalyptic in the history of architectural preservation, as can be seen in the destruction of Manhattan's Pennsylvania Station. The tide of public interest in historic properties had receded just before a demand for preservation emerged after 1963.

Five decades have passed since The Point came into the stewardship of the New York State Office of Parks, Recreation and Historic Preservation, which has entertained many potential uses of the site and its declining structure. In 1974, the house was listed on the National Register of Historic Places, and in 2008, the Calvert Vaux Preservation Alliance was formed with the mission of preserving the architect's legacy in the Hudson Valley. Grants for stabilization have been awarded by the State Environmental Protection Fund and Save America's Treasures, but this unrivaled architectural landmark is now in need of further restoration funding.

———

**OPPOSITE** Calvert Vaux chose weathered stone for the house's exterior. **ABOVE** The entrance hall was reimagined by Robert Palmer Huntington to include classical architectural references. **RIGHT** The upstairs hall still retains Calvert Vaux's signature-canted doorheads. Vaux wrote, "The hall is amply lighted and is roomy and open, which is desideratum in the country."

NORTHWOOD

1856

THE FIFTH AND MOST NORTHERN portion of the land division that took place after the death of Robert "The Chancellor" Livingston's daughter Elizabeth and the subsequent 1843 death of her husband, Edward Philip Livingston, was the allotment that went to their son Robert Edward Livingston. Fittingly, here he built Northwood, one of many consecutive country seats in the subdivisions initiated by Elizabeth's will. Upon his brother Clermont's inheritance of the eponymously named estate, Robert Edward stayed on, living in the south wing of the house until he married his neighbor and cousin, Susan de Peyster, and started planning Northwood, their own home. During the construction, they lived in their New York City townhouse located at 271 Fifth Avenue at Twenty-ninth Street. Their purchase of several large contiguous farms in Germantown assembled the largest estate on Woods Road.

Like the other Livingston's houses along Woods Road, Northwood is perched on a hillock with commanding views of the river. Designed by architect William Baldwin Stewart, Northwood exhibits a robust Renaissance Revival style, and boasts the de rigueur Second Empire mansard roofline so popular at the time.

Robert Edward's youngest son, Goodhue Livingston, a partner in the New York architectural firm of Trowbridge and Livingston, was responsible for later improvements to the house as well as several of the outbuildings. Catering to a well-heeled clientele, his firm went on to design and build the St. Regis Hotel in 1904, B. Altman &

Company Department Store in 1905, J. P. Morgan and Company's headquarters on Wall Street in 1913, and the Hayden Planetarium at the American Museum of Natural History in 1935.

Eventually, toward the end of the nineteenth century, the house passed on to Goodhue's nephew, Robert "Reggie" Reginald, newly elected to the New York State Assembly. Reggie was passionate about horticulture and agriculture, and greatly improved the orchards. He was responsible for one of the state's first cold-storage facilities for fruit and purchased the Stone Jug, a splendid 1757 Palatine stone house, on Route 9G, which became part of the estate at this time.

In 1967, Willard and Ripley Golovin were guests of Howland and Frances Davis at Teviot. During this visit they intended to follow up on an announcement at an earlier dinner that Dorothy—Reggie's secretary, second wife, and eventually his widow—was putting Northwood up for sale. Howland took the Golovins to Northwood, where he had grown up, after visiting neighboring Orlot, Edgewater, and Clermont. The romance of the region intoxicated the newcomers, and they became the first family without a Livingston pedigree to own Northwood.

Willard ran a highly successful advertising agency in New York City whose clients included Harry Winston, Elizabeth Arden, and Lanvin. He also owned the Bayer Gallery, which sold Henri Matisse and Hans Hofmann's art as well as the work of many of the Abstract Expressionists with whom he had painted earlier as a student at the Art Students League of New York. In many cases, the art and furnishings in the house are the fruits of extensive auction visits and forays that Willard made into the local countryside antiques shops with his wife and daughter, who both shared the name Ripley.

Ripley Golovin Hathaway and her husband, Tyler, inherited Northwood in 1992. She reminisces about the brutal winters when the Golovins' 1967 Town & Country station wagon, which incon-

PREVIOUS SPREAD Northwood's mansard roof rests on heavy brackets and is accentuated by windows with Renaissance Revival details. OPPOSITE The elevated veranda, oriented toward the Hudson River, surrounds three sides of the house and serves as a popular place where the Hathaway family gathers. ABOVE An 1855 pen and gouache rendering of the house is signed by architect William Baldwin Stewart.

ABOVE Nineteenth-century paintings from the Hudson River School hang above the bar. OPPOSITE An early nineteenth-century Italian marble mantel in the parlor came from an earlier family home on Washington Square in Manhattan.

veniently only had front-wheel drive, could not make the trip down the steep hill. The family would then use sleds to transport themselves from the carriage house with their weekend suitcases and groceries to the main house.

"Big Ripley" and "Little Ripley" often hosted bridge games at Northwood with Clermont's Honoria Livingston McVitty, who made the weekly jaunt up Woods Road to join in with her husband, Rex, and local historian and raconteuse Squeaky Hatch. The Northwood bridge game became a tradition and is often still played in the parlor, where guests from the nearby Edgewood Club

gather during the winter when the club is closed for the season.

Photograph albums were included with the sale of the house to the Golovins illustrating the nineteenth- and early twentieth-century country life, which was intimate and poetic in nature. Numerous images of the family in the orchards, skiing down the steep abyss leading to the Hudson, and riding atop an iceboat, which would be brought down to the river once it had frozen solid, depicted a family busy entertaining large groups and making full use of the grounds.

To celebrate the family's fiftieth year of ownership, the Hathaways hosted a party in July 2017, making clear the expectation that guests come appropriately dressed in attire from the late 1960s. Bell-bottoms, Pucci shifts, and Lilly Pulitzer outfits covered the front lawn. The guests who were amassed in front of the house provided the opportunity to reflect on past gatherings and mirrored many of the house parties previously and so eloquently captured in the photograph albums.

---

**OPPOSITE** One of a pair of framed mirrors, commissioned by Willard Golovin in the 1960s, reflects light into the entrance hall and hangs above a contemporary harpsichord. **ABOVE** The dining room's fireplace mantel was carved from a fallen oak tree on the property.

# OBERCREEK

## 1856

THE NAME OBERCREEK WAS GIVEN TO the southernmost Livingston home on the Hudson River by Mary Augusta Willis Reese. The property crosses Wappinger Creek in the tiny hamlet of Hughsonville, just south of Poughkeepsie. Alex Reese, a great-grandson of Mary Augusta and her husband William Henry, is the present steward of the property along with his wife, architect Alison Spear.

Recent family anecdotes carry the narrative of the house into the twenty-first century. One such tale unfolds during a period when Alex needed to secure an architect to update the family home he inherited with his siblings in 2003 from their parents, Willis Livingston Mesier Reese and his wife, Frances, known as "Franny." At a dinner in New York City that year given by their mutual friend Katie Ford, Alex found himself seated next to Alison. By the end of the evening professional, as well as personal, sparks began to fly between them.

Alex was living nearby at Edge Hill, a Greek Revival house that had remained in his family for many generations. He was both dreading and looking forward to commencing a major facelift to Obercreek, which had been in a direct line of family ownership for

---

**PREVIOUS SPREAD** Alison Spear reduced the massing of the third floor to create the cupola effect, which references an earlier version of the house. **ABOVE** The chapel was added in the 1920s by Alex Reese's grandmother. It was constructed in red oak by Gleb Derujinsky, who also designed the Colonial Revival front portico of the house. **RIGHT** The entrance hall is lined with family portraits.

six generations. "Alex, as a highly intelligent man with an astute business mind, knew that marrying an architect and designer would have its benefits." This was pronounced at the couple's wedding in 2007 by his niece. The benefits are apparent upon visiting the recently reconsidered home. Historic collections with their provenance are a rare and spectacular occurrence, but sometimes a fresh eye can be transformational in their placement.

The central hall, which is paved in the original marble tiles brought over from Italy in the 1850s, is hung with an impressive collection of family portraits. Alison moved them from every corner of the house to hang shoulder to shoulder, creating a striking welcome. This new installation was met with resistance from Alex, whose attachments to where things had previously been placed was countered with an insouciant "Why not?" And, there in the hall the pictures stayed.

"We intended the result of the redesign to be absolutely something that was new and about us," said Alison. The architectural difficulty in rethinking an immense home that had been improved through many iterations was met head on. Alex explains that "the house always had a delineation between the public and private service spaces, even insofar as how one navigated the rooms. We wanted to obliterate those feelings and philosophy while still preserving the axial views and relationships of the rooms." Therefore, the top floor, which was composed of a rabbit warren of service rooms, was reduced in size creating a more harmonious composition. The house now appears less top heavy. Alison adds, "No one that we know lives in a house with staff. We didn't want a grand house that we couldn't take care of or maintain on a budget in the future."

To reconcile an odd connection between two wings on the west elevation, Alison added a forty-foot-long dining veranda that takes advantage of the views of the Catskill Mountains. A daring unexpected modernist garage containing an exercise studio was added, off grid with the house, as a freestanding structure. Using vintage bricks that were laid in part to duplicate patterns visible in the original house, an unconventional relationship was created between the two seemingly disparate buildings.

When Alex's mother, Franny, died in 2003, her five children created an exhaustive list of what they wanted from Obercreek. Alex sold Edge Hill and bought out his siblings' interests in the Obercreek house. The remainder was auctioned off on-site under a tent, with the proceeds, approaching 500,000 dollars, turned over to Scenic Hudson, one of several preservation groups in which Franny was deeply involved.

Gilbert Livingston, whose portrait graces the entrance to Obercreek's hall, came south to Poughkeepsie from Columbia County in the middle of the eighteenth century to make his fortune on land sales previously belonging to the Wapani Indians. Gilbert's son Henry, Sr., moved from Poughkeepsie and built his residence close to the banks of the Hudson. He made a gift of a large tract of

---

**ABOVE** The comfortable living room is filled with assorted family furnishings and portraits. **OPPOSITE ABOVE** The bookcases in the library are original to the room. The William IV desk sits on a reed and leather Tuareg rug from Morocco. **OPPOSITE BELOW** The dining room walls are painted a deep burnt orange.

land to his son Henry, Jr., on the occasion of his marriage in 1771 when he built his own home, naming it Locust Grove. Here, he worked as a land surveyor and wrote poetry. Henry, Jr., is credited by two of Dutchess County's revered historians, Benson J. Lossing and Helen Wilkinson Reynolds, with the 1805 composition of *A Visit from Saint Nicholas*, which begins "T'was the night before Christmas." In the mid-1800s the noted painter and inventor Samuel F. B. Morse purchased the home of Henry, Sr., and hired A. J. Davis to transform it into an Italianate villa, also naming it Locust Grove.

In 1850, William Henry Willis built Carnwath nearby in the Wheeler Hill Historic District; the building presently houses the Frances Reese Cultural Center, owned and administered by the Town of Wappinger. Saddened by the death of his son in 1856, Willis decided to sell Carnwath and purchased William Hughson's neighboring Federal house, which he vastly expanded in the Italianate style. It was when William Henry's daughter, Mary Augusta, inherited the house that it was named Obercreek. To complicate matters, she married another William Henry, with the surname Reese. It is through this line that the connection to Gilbert Livingston is maintained.

Through six generations, Obercreek and its landholdings have waxed and waned, beginning with 100 acres when it was purchased in 1856, peaking at 350 acres, and now covering 240 acres. Over time each family member, as steward, adapted the house to the needs of his or her generation.

The property was a dairy farm until the 1960s. Alison and Alex reintroduced this agricultural component by creating a community-supported co-op, Obercreek Farm. Now sheep and goats roam the fields next to solar greenhouses, where vegetables are grown, and the Obercreek Brewing Company produces beer, which includes local farm-grown hops. Alex explains that the goal is to "bring the community onto the property, bolster the decreasing agricultural history of the area, and give some meaning to the property and navigate it toward sustainability."

---

**LEFT** The dining porch was added in 2007 and connects the north and south wings of the ground floor. **ABOVE** Spear designed the off-grid modernist building, using reclaimed bricks. It houses the gym and garage, replacing a former one-story clapboard structure.

CHIDDINGSTONE

1860

THE CURIOUS NAME OF CHIDDINGSTONE can be traced to the ancestral lands of writer Thomas Streatfeild Clarkson III, who built this house in 1860. Most of the town of Chiddingstone, in Kent, England, is now owned by the National Trust. There lies England's most picturesque inn, built in 1420. The Streatfeilds had been majority landowners in the town since 1584 and in the 1800s, they built Chiddingstone Castle over the footprint of a previous Tudor manor house. The legendary chiding stone is located in the center of the village. Historically, husbands brought their nagging and offending wives for punishment, or chiding, to this spot. The roots for this practice may trace back to a Druid rock that is still present in the town.

The land on which Chiddingstone was built in Germantown had passed from Chancellor Robert Livingston to his granddaughter Margaret through her mother, Elizabeth. Here, Margaret constructed a house in 1845 with her husband, David Augustus Clarkson, and upon his death in 1850, she divided the property between her two children. Her daughter, Elizabeth, inherited the property where Ridgely currently is situated, and her son, Thomas Streatfeild Clarkson III, was given Chiddingstone, his parents' house.

Upon his marriage to Mary Whitmarsh in 1855, Thomas Streatfeild Clarkson III tore down his parents' house and built the present home in the Bracketed Italianate style, integrated with heavy late Georgian elements. The home is characterized by numerous bold brackets supporting the entablature, cornices, and the square columns of the porches. The squared, symmetrical plan is representational of late Georgian high-style architecture, with details that include four projecting pavilions with triangular pediments, Palladian windows, and quoined corners.

The Chiddingstone property originally included Clermont Farms, across Woods Road. This horse-breeding establishment appealed to the 1950s owners, who were accountants involved with organized crime, because the stables created a cover for their business endeavors. It was understood that if the limousine was parked sideways across the driveway, no one was to enter.

Christina Mohr and Matt Guerreiro, who both work in finance, purchased the house in 1991 after the property languished on the market for four years and embarked on an overhaul. A renovation project of this scale took courage but the fifteen-foot ceilings intoxicated the new owners.

The couple gradually decided on a composition with an aesthetic that was true to the home's historic fabric. They enlisted the professional wisdom of their immediate neighbors Carey Maloney and Hermes Mallea of M (Group) Design. Maloney remarked, "When you have a Texan (Maloney) and a Cuban (Mallea) working on a project, there is no fear of scale. We weren't daunted by the height of the ceilings—they were a joy."

---

**PREVIOUS SPREAD** Left: The Chiddingstone dining porch offers a spectacular view of the Catskill Mountains. Right: Architects Carey Maloney and Hermes Mallea of M (Group) studied many Livingston houses for design inspiration before replacing the demolished veranda. The new one wraps around three sides of the Georgian Revival house. **LEFT** The library's paneling was installed in the 1920s using wood from the property's trees. A collection of turquoise pottery sits on the mantel beneath a New Guinea ceremonial cape.

PREVIOUS SPREAD A Knole sofa faces a mid-nineteenth-century fireplace in the living room and sits on an antique Chinese rug, setting the tone for Carey Maloney's trademark eclectic mix. RIGHT The dining room was designed around a large Agra carpet decorated with birds and flowers. Renowned colorist Donald Kaufman created the palette for the house's interiors.

Maloney designed handsome parlors that integrate and complement the bold original moldings and the dark wood trim. The wood paneling in the library is said to have been added in the 1920s using a fallen tree from the property. Most of the furnishings were sourced nearby in the town of Hudson, several miles to the north, which has evolved into a mecca for eclectic antiques stores, auction galleries, and cultural activities. "We didn't need to go to New York or Paris. This was a local project," says Maloney.

After a period of reflection, Mallea moved the kitchen to the first floor. In the 1930s, to remedy the lack of natural light penetrating the windows in the basement kitchen, the wraparound porch had been removed to appease the discontented chef, who was unable to cook due to the poor natural lighting. Once the kitchen was beautifully sun-drenched, the porch begged to be reinstated.

Following a comprehensive series of visits to neighboring homes of the same period along the Hudson River, plans were drawn up by Mallea, synthesizing the best elements they had encountered. The addition of the porch has taken the property back to its original 1860 appearance, creating spectacular opportunities to better experience the river.

ABOVE Positioned to maximize the views of the river, the master bedroom is furnished with an Aesthetic Movement sofa that is paired with multiple Middle Eastern tabourets. LEFT AND OPPOSITE The original office was replaced with the recently installed sun-filled kitchen. The chandelier above the kitchen table came with the house, as did most of the other lighting fixtures.

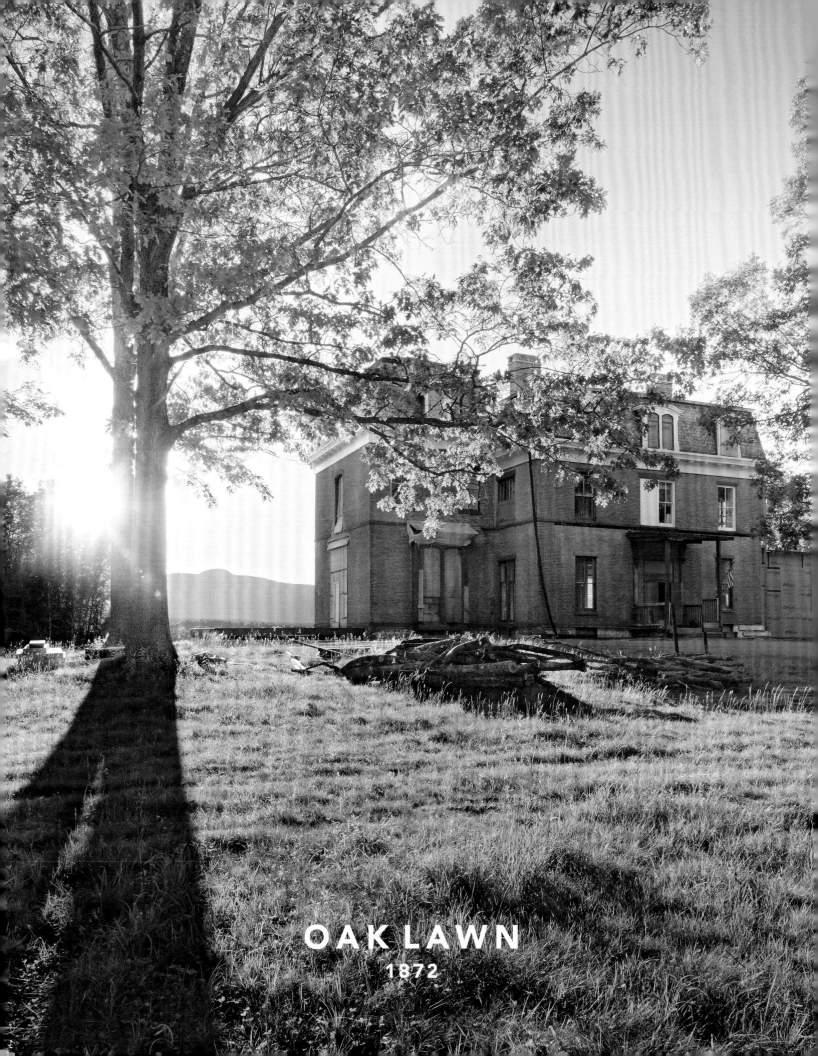

OAK LAWN

1872

TWO LUDLOW SIBLINGS MARRIED two Hall siblings in the early 1860s, and in a gesture ripe with novelty, decided to move next door to one another on Woods Road in Tivoli. Mary Livingston Ludlow and Valentine Gill Hall, Jr., were the builders of Oak Lawn, as it was originally named to twin with its neighbor Pine Lawn. The couple enlisted the architect Carl Pfeiffer, who was to go on to design the Fifth Avenue Presbyterian Church in 1874. The only previous commission Pfeiffer had received in America after emigrating from Germany when he was sixteen was the Metropolitan Savings Bank Building, across from The Cooper Union in 1867. This building served as inspiration for the Halls' home. Designed in the Second Empire style that had become fashionable in Paris during the rule of Napoleon III, Oak Lawn was completed in 1872. Valentine's sister Margaret Hall married Edward Philip Livingston Ludlow, Mary's brother, and lived at Pine Lawn and contributed to the family's genealogy, which had evolved into a complex Gordian knot.

Eleanor Roosevelt, a descendant of Robert "The Chancellor" Livingston, grew up at Oak Lawn with her brother, Gracie Hall Roosevelt. Eleanor's mother had died when her daughter was eight, and her father, Elliott, passed away the following year from acute alcoholism. As a result, Eleanor was brought up by her grandparents Mary and Valentine Gill Hall, Jr., at Oak Lawn in Germantown and at their townhouse at 11 West Thirty-seventh Street in Manhattan.

In 1884 a meeting was held at Oak Lawn to organize and establish bylaws for the nation's first tennis and golf association, the Edgewood Club of Tivoli. The club is still going strong 134 years after having been established as a family gathering place. The use of the word "family" did not refer to the inclusion of children, but rather to the specific family, the Livingstons, who were responsible for initiating memberships. The meeting at Oak Lawn was attended by Livingston cousins with the intention to create an environment where they could battle out their differences on the courts and fairways. Eugene Livingston, who lived at Teviot, donated a parcel of land for the club, now discreetly tucked into the woods on property owned by the family 332 years ago. The porch of the spartan original clubhouse is still the location for Saturday teas at four o'clock that are hosted by members during the season.

Eleanor's uncles Valentine Hall III and his brother Edward were spectacular tennis players and cut dashing figures in their white summer flannels. In keeping with other family members, Valentine's relationship with alcohol, just like his brother-in-law Elliott Roosevelt's, was to be his downfall, literally in several cases. In a daze he reportedly had plunged eighteen feet to the first floor after miscalculating how high the balustrade of the first-floor landing had been. After inheriting Oak Lawn, Valentine became infamous for resting his shotgun on the sill of his bedroom window, waiting like a hunter for a bear, or for unsuspecting visitors or merchants to approach the house after transporting themselves past the stylistically identical gatehouse, where the housekeeper lived, and down the mile-long driveway. By the front door a sign was posted, which instructed, "If you can't find me, fire gun." By 1934, the Halls had vacated the house entirely.

In Newport, Rhode Island, the houses had ballrooms, but on the Hudson, they had libraries. Eleanor, who was a passionate reader,

ABOVE The enfilade of connecting reception rooms faces west
BELOW The restoration of the entrance hall is designed to preserve
the original details. OPPOSITE The pastoral view from Oak Lawn
has remained unspoiled since the house was built in the 1870s.

found herself constantly occupied with her grandparents' extensive collection of books and manuscripts. It was reported that she had read them in their entirety by the time she was twelve, shortly before choosing to attend the Allenswood School in London to finish her studies and escape the strict discipline and confines of her elderly guardians. She spent time canoeing on the Hudson River and riding her horse-drawn carriage two miles into town to visit her close friend Carola de Peyster, who was living at the Château de Tivoli. In her autobiography *This is My Story*, she wrote "My brother and I thought it a very amusing thing to climb out of the window and walk around on the gutter to a window on the other side of the house. We were caught and informed that the gutter was made of tin and might easily have broken under our weight; besides, it was just the grace of heaven that we did not fall off, when we certainly should have been killed." Eleanor married her fifth cousin Franklin Delano Roosevelt in 1905 and went on to become a formidable First Lady, philanthropist, and cultivator of Dutchess County traditions with Val-Kill Industries, which specialized in making furniture, pewter, and homespun cloth modeled on local eighteenth-century forms.

Van Lamprou purchased Oak Lawn on twenty-six acres and moved up to the area after selling Dolce Vita Footwear in 2013. "The house certainly has presence," notes Van. "I knew I wouldn't get too many chances to do this. It leaves me with an elevated sense of purpose." Whether or not there was a complete understanding of the immense scope of work ahead remains to be seen. At 8,375 square feet, this is the behemoth of restoration projects. The terrace with its balustrade is presently being reconstructed to surround the entire first floor. The new kitchen wing, which is roughly based on the steel and glass Crystal Palace that was the centerpiece of the Great Exhibition of 1851 in London, is slowly evolving. Several of the original eighteen marble fireplaces are remaining and are being refitted. One begins to see that Lamprou is not one to set the bar of success within easy reach.

Currently living nearby with his wife, Kimberly, and two daughters, Lexie and Gabrielle, Van participates actively in the renovation of the buff-colored brick house and its grounds. The scale of the project is daunting as is the scale of the eighteen-foot-high living room ceiling. The second floor has sixteen-foot ceilings and the third is fourteen-foot high, so when standing on top of the mansard roof, the view is one of the most impressive in an area which has prided itself for centuries on superlative vistas of the Catskill Mountains. The Lamprous have taken on this immense project with the firm intention of creating a space that pays homage to Eleanor and her values. Their intention is to have a portion of the house made available to nonprofit organizations, which embrace Eleanor's ideas of humanity, civic engagement, and community contribution. "I hope I can have people here to inspire them to do more," says Lamprou.

Eleanor reflected often on her experiences at Oak Terrace, as she called Oak Lawn. In 1940, she wrote in her ubiquitous column "My Day": "The house looks very much neglected, and for many years nobody has done much to the grounds except cut down some trees. Still, as we sat and ate our picnic supper, watching the sun go down behind the Catskill Mountains, I could not help feeling a sense of beauty and peace. It may be sad to return to the scene of one's childhood and realize all the things that have happened in the intervening years to the people one loves; yet there is also something very sweet in remembering the good things which no sadness can wipe out."

IN 1858, WILLIAM BACKHOUSE ASTOR, JR., acknowledged at that time as the son of the wealthiest man in the country, purchased 105 acres near Rokeby, the home owned by his parents, William Backhouse Astor, Sr., and Margaret Armstrong Astor. Margaret's mother was Alida Schuyler Livingston, a daughter of Robert "The Judge" Livingston. The Astor fortune was recent compared to that of the Livingstons, but it was massive and had enabled the family's rapid social and financial ascent.

John Jacob Astor, the progenitor of the family's wealth, immigrated to America with empty pockets in 1784 from Walldorf, Germany, after a short sojourn in England. By 1820, his business, the American Fur Company, had a virtual monopoly on fur trading east of the Rocky Mountains. He invested his earnings in Manhattan real estate, zealously assembling a portfolio based out of his early residence and office at 149 Broadway.

On his property, William built a large Italianate house, called Ferncliff, for himself and his wife, Caroline Schermerhorn Astor, based on architect Griffith Thomas's plans. The couple also had a home in LaGrange Terrace, now known as Colonnade Row, on Lafayette Place in New York City, which housed assorted Astors and Delanos behind its august Greek Revival facade.

After raising five children, William and Caroline settled into separate lives. She firmly established herself as a supremely ambitious matriarch, defining New York society at the dawn of the Gilded Age. As the frenzy of social competition increased toward the end of the nineteenth century, stopgap measures were implemented by Caroline Astor and Ward McAllister who famously coined the phrase "The Four Hundred," referring to the number of select guests able to fit in Mrs. Astor's ballroom.

Caroline ruled New York society from the couple's home on Fifth Avenue and Thirty-fourth Street. The house was sold and after several decades as the Astoria Hotel became the site of the Empire State Building. Her next project was to commission architect Richard Morris Hunt to design a French Renaissance–style château at 840 Fifth Avenue at Sixty-fifth Street with an even larger ballroom.

Ferncliff was the place William quickly escaped to in an effort to get away from the stress associated with his undesired place in society. Despite membership in the city's most exclusive social institution, the Patriarchs, his interests lay in farming, raising horses, and traveling on his steam yacht. William's brother, John Jacob Astor III, was quoted as saying, "Money brings me nothing but a certain dull anxiety," perhaps overstating the ennui that had already set in after a third generation of extreme wealth.

Ferncliff's property was elaborately described in James H. Smith's illustrious book, *The History of Dutchess County*, published in 1882, as being "so lavishly improved artificially that it is now justly ranked as one of the most attractive and desirable country-seats upon the Hudson . . . It may be said that it is planned upon a scale of magnificence and furnished with a degree of luxuriousness, perfectly in keeping with its outward surroundings." Upon entering beneath a massive stone portico supported by Corinthian columns, a visitor

---

Landscape designer Louis Augustus Ehlers designed Ferncliff Lodge for William Backhouse Astor, Jr., to serve as a sentry on River Road in Rhinebeck, while offering the visitor a preview of Ferncliff's magnificent pleasure grounds.

# FERNCLIFF LODGE

## 1879

Artists Lois Guarino and Stan Lichens use the outbuildings on the property as their painting and photography studios.

---

passed through to a spacious hall, then continued into a vestibule before arriving onto the veranda, with one of the "grandest views" across the Hudson. At the bottom of the path leading to the river, Astor's yacht *The Ambassadress* was moored, then considered the largest and most magnificently appointed yacht in the world.

Hans Jacob Ehlers was chosen by Astor to oversee the property's accumulation of several local farms and aggregate them into a finely landscaped gentleman's retreat. He had arrived in America around 1841 from Germany with his six-year-old son, Louis Augustus. Ehlers had been well trained in arboriculture and the early English Romantic landscaping philosophy of Humphry Repton and John Claudius Loudon at the Forest Academy in Kiel. He made his way up the Hudson initially to find work at Rokeby, then owned by Astor's father. The many symmetrical flowerbeds that Ehlers laid in the lawn there created a very pleasing environment, and were considered a masterpiece of nineteenth-century landscaping.

Louis Augustus Ehlers designed and built Ferncliff Lodge in 1879, using repurposed materials that had been left over from the construction of the main house. It became his home and also functioned as a gatehouse. The Second Empire structure was clad with massive rough-faced ashlar of cut granite, identical to the

connecting property walls, and supports an impressive polychromatic mansard roof. Originally, there was a stone canopy with a copper roof that extended onto two chamfered stone piers where the structure connected to the gate, removed sometime during the 1930s. The section of the wall running north of Ferncliff Lodge was donated by Brooke Astor in 1959 for the building of the Rhinebeck High School, during the period in which she shepherded the property out of the family.

The carriage road, which led to the main house, was nearly a mile long, and was "kept in the most perfect condition . . . and here assumes the character of a private drive through an extensive park," according to *The History of Dutchess County*. The Misses Astor were reported to have been driving their pony phaeton on East Market Street in Rhinebeck in 1876 when they collided with "Lewis Livingston, who chaperoned them back to the extensive parterres, sweeping lawns, and conservatories which dotted the landscape of Ferncliff."

John Jacob Astor IV, son of William Backhouse, Jr., inherited Ferncliff in 1892. He took possession with his first wife, Ava Lowle Willing, and their infant son, William Vincent, who was known by his middle name. Ava considered the house a huge white elephant, and Gore Vidal reported, "Once when a guest was leaving, he thanked Ava for a splendid weekend and wondered what on earth he could do to repay her hospitality. 'On the way out,' she said in her deep Edwardian voice, 'drop a match.'" In 1894, John Jacob penned *A Journey in Other Worlds* in which he described a fantastic future in the year 2000 aboard the spaceship *Callisto*.

John Jacob and Ava commissioned architect Stanford White to design the Ferncliff Casino in 1902, which was completed in 1906. The sports complex, with the first heated indoor pool in the country, covered tennis and squash courts, a barbershop, and a bowling alley, as well as four bedrooms, was conceived in a majestic style, even for White. The inspiration for White was architect Jules Hardouin-Mansart's Grand Trianon at Versailles.

Vincent Astor came into his vast inheritance, including Ferncliff, at age twenty following his father's drowning while on the maiden voyage of the *Titanic* in 1912. John Jacob Astor IV's body was retrieved from Halifax and brought back to Rhinebeck, where his funeral was held at the family's place of worship, the Church of the Messiah. His father's still-ticking gold pocket watch became the most cherished object of this young, modern Croesus. Several years later, Vincent's brother-in-law, Prince Serge Obolensky, remarked that "the demands of taking care of one of the greatest fortunes in the world was literally overpowering."

Vincent began conversations regarding the improvement of the Ferncliff Creamery and agricultural complex in 1917 with architect Harrie T. Lindeberg, who had recently completed Foxhollow Farm, a few miles to the south. Thomas Wolfe used Ferncliff as a model for the "Paston estate" in his novel *Of Time and the River* and described in detail the exuberant fireworks display he experienced there on the banks of the Hudson River. Architect Charles A. Platt, who had been designated by Astor to complete the project, finished construction of the barns and outbuildings in 1918. The French Provincial design of the complex created a whimsical counterpoint to the geometric severity of the Casino and ironically echoed back to the rural charms of Marie-Antoinette's Hameau de la Reine, also at Versailles.

The main house at Ferncliff was torn down immediately following Vincent's second marriage in 1940 to Mary "Minnie" Cushing. Vincent's first wife had been neighbor Helen Dinsmore Huntington, and Minnie felt the house held too many memories of her predecessor. In keeping with the trend to downsize, the demolition of Ferncliff followed that of Vincent's grandmother's Fifth Avenue home in 1926, which made way for Temple Emanu-El.

Many pieces of salvaged material were collected from the ruins of Ferncliff and made their way into subsequent homes. The magnificent parquet floor and Swedish pine paneling were appropriated by Jerome Zerbe, a frequent guest of the Astors and the society editor of *Vanity Fair*, for his 1948 Connecticut home, Windsong. Following the demolition of the main house, the Casino became the principal residence of the Astors.

As the publisher of *Newsweek* starting in 1937, Vincent had the resources to indulge a passion for printing mock newspapers. Vidal described an incident one weekend, "To give him due credit, he had an ingeniously malevolent sense of humor. For one of his houseguests, a lady notorious for her gallantry, he prepared a special edition of a Hearst Sunday newspaper. The details of her love life were on three, provoking a most satisfying set of hysterics." Vincent's developed "farm-to-table" philosophy made its way to his St. Regis Hotel. Reflecting daily transport from Ferncliff's hennery, the hotel menu bore the proud claim that "no egg served at the St. Regis is more than twenty-four hours old."

As an active member of the Edgewood Club, Vincent invited members to play tennis in the Casino's covered courts when inclement weather arrived. His dear friend Franklin Delano Roosevelt was a frequent guest, especially following his polio diagnosis, as the indoor pool offered privacy and excellent exercise for the motivated future president.

After Vincent died in 1959, his third wife, Brooke, gifted the riverfront portion of Ferncliff to the Roman Catholic Archdiocese of New York as a tax deduction after trying unsuccessfully to market and sell the immense property. In 1959, the white elephant was offered for sale on 2,800 acres along with dozens of historic structures. Jim and Mary McGuire purchased part of the estate from the church and lived in the Casino before moving into the Tea House, a folly on the property. The neighboring Ferncliff Forest was donated by Brooke Astor to the Rhinebeck Rotary Club to be kept in perpetuity as a forest preserve.

Today, artists Stan Lichens and his wife, Lois Guarino, live in the gatehouse with their daughter, Livi. Louis Augustus Ehlers's original design for this part of the farm included three graperies, rose and carnation houses, a large flowering-plant house and a surviving conservatory that is still maintained adjacent to the home, near the couple's art studios.

Stan and Lois saw the gatehouse while exploring the area in 1987. They spoke with a Realtor in Rhinebeck on a whim and requested listings of houses for future consideration. The next day the telephone rang and they were informed that the lodge, which they had not specifically mentioned to the Realtor, was for sale. Upon inspection, they saw that the uninhabited gatehouse was dilapidated and an extremely challenging fit for their young family. After enduring a rigorous two-year vetting process by the seller, which included numerous teas at the historic Beekman Arms in Rhinebeck, their offer was accepted and they took possession in 1989.

**ABOVE** Ferncliff as seen in 1914. **BELOW** Ferncliff Casino, inspired by the Grand Trianon at Versailles, was designed by Stanford White in 1902 as a recreation center for the family and their guests. It went on to serve as the principal residence for Vincent Astor following Ferncliff's demolition in the early 1940s.

HOLCROFT

1881

A FIRST TOUR OF HOLCROFT, if the visitor is lucky enough to be accompanied by the present owner and Livingston descendent, Eliot Hawkins, is a *Cliffs Notes* shortcut to the story of his family. The walls in the house are covered with the past: family portraits, framed personal letters, and items pertaining to the long period the Hawkinses have been based along this stretch of the Hudson River. The home has remained in the family since it was originally built in the mid-1840s in the Carpenter Gothic style. The line of the home's ownership started in 1843, when upon the death of Edward P. Livingston, at Clermont, the land was given to his daughter Elizabeth, who had married Edward Hunter Ludlow in 1833. Edward Philip's sister Mary Livingston Ludlow married Valentine Hall, Margaret Hall's brother, and built Oak Lawn next door.

In 1879, the original wooden house, named Pine Lawn, burned to the ground as a result of embers falling from a passing train onto a pile of dead leaves. The nearby trains that separated the homes from the Hudson had become the family's nemesis. The new home was intentionally constructed in brick by Edward Philip Livingston Ludlow and his wife, Margaret Hall, in 1881 so as not to bring about a similar fate. In 1890, he added a billiards room, today the parlor, on the back of the house. During this period, a total of eight structures, including barns and sheds, were sited on the property. Holcroft was purchased in 1904 by Howard and

PREVIOUS SPREAD Left: The Hawkins family collection of Livingston memorabilia is displayed along the staircase walls of Holcroft. Right: A glimpse of the Hudson River from the parlor. LEFT The proximity to the river distinguishes Holcroft from its Livingston neighbors on Woods Road in Germantown. ABOVE The neatly trimmed boxwoods that line the escarpment leading to the river were planted by present owner Paula Hawkins.

Alice Delafield Clarkson. Alice was a second cousin of the Ludlows and the great-grandmother of the present owner. The Clarksons changed the name of the house to Holcroft, which was the maiden name of Clarkson's English ancestor, Elizabeth Holcroft Clarkson.

In 1905, the Clarksons moved in and immediately relocated the front door from the river side to the north, and redirected the driveway. Alice also laid out the formal gardens on the south side of the property with the assistance of her daughter and namesake, Alice Delafield Clarkson, who soon married her cousin John Henry Livingston in 1906 and moved into his home, Clermont.

In 1930, the house was left to Cornelia Livingston Clarkson, "Great-Aunt Nelly," by her mother, the elder Alice Delafield Clarkson. Cornelia sold the gatehouse on five acres before leaving Holcroft to the present owner, Eliot Hawkins.

Hawkins's familiarity with this region runs deep. As a child he remembers playing Sardines, a form of hide-and-seek, when he congregated with his cousins under sheets covering the furniture at Holcroft, the home of his great-aunt. Holdcroft was a few miles north of Wildercliff, where he spent summers with his grandmother Julia Clarkson Hawkins in Rhinebeck. His memories of the house and grounds, which are rooted in the 1930s, are still crisp and spectacularly well delivered.

With muslin still protecting the furniture and paintings, Eliot began his stewardship of the property in 1968 upon inheriting Holcroft. With his wife, Paula, he now spends weekends and summers at the house, located on Woods Road, and weekdays in New York where he had worked as a trust and estates attorney at the firm of Milbank, Tweed, Hadley & McCloy.

Eliot is a rare repository of Livingston history. He is one of the few who remembers firsthand many of the stories revolving around a family blessed with an array of personalities and characters. Several of these are captured in Clermont State Historic Site's newly released film documenting its history, with Eliot filling in many of the blanks with his valued recollections.

---

**ABOVE** An enthusiasm for riding and all things equestrian is evident throughout the house. **RIGHT** The billiards table that dominates the entrance hall came from Clermont.

The portrait on the left is of Julia Floyd Delafield. Hanging above the fireplace is a nineteenth-century copy of the original 1804 portrait of Robert "The Chancellor" Livingston that was painted in Paris by John Vanderlyn. Robert, along with his brother Edward, had financed Vanderlyn's trip to Europe so that he might obtain copies of old master paintings and casts of antique sculpture to bring back to the American Academy of the Fine Arts in Manhattan. The portrait on the right is of "Aunt Pinkie," painted by her father, Charles Baker.

MIDWOOD

1887

IF THE CAMP MIDWOOD T-SHIRTS mounted on the third-floor wall of Joan Davidson's house in Germantown don't say it all about tradition and family connection, then they certainly say a good deal about these values. Joan established "Camp Midwood," in 1995, for her grandchildren to gather during the summer for several weeks to enjoy camplike activities. The fact that this is a family house is reinforced through multiple lunches, dinners, and spectacular events held on the front lawn overlooking the Hudson River.

The contrast between formality and informality that marks this household harkens back to country residences from the time of Midwood's construction in 1888. Visits here bring warm introductions to Joan's relatives, and when one believes that the entire family has been presented, another relation magically appears.

Midwood was built following the division of neighboring Southwood into two parcels intended for the children of Mary Livingston and Levinus Clarkson. The construction of the house on the footprint of Southwood's garden house began immediately after the marriage of their second son, Robert Livingston Clarkson, to Mary Otis in 1886. Mary and her stunningly attractive sister Martha, who became involved in a "French arrangement" with the Prince de Polignac, were both protégées of Ward McAllister and were included on "The Four Hundred," his list that was the exclusive social register of the time.

Architect Michael O'Connor crafted the house in the popular Colonial Revival style of the late nineteenth century. The name Midwood referred to its cozy position—sandwiched between Southwood and Northwood. In fact, there was a shared entrance drive until 1912, when the entrance to Midwood became independent.

An avid equestrian, Robert was known as the only man who could take a four-in-hand through the neighboring gate at Chiddingstone at a trot. Curiously, he was never able to drive a car, but his chauffeur, Chester Loonie, true to his name, maniacally escorted him in his Graham-Paige roadster. The shared private road, where Robert practiced but never mastered driving by himself, connected all of the cousins' homes along Woods Road through this path, which was convenient for family visits.

Mary and Levinus's youngest daughter, Pauline, or "Polly," married married Frank Washburn at St. Paul's Church in Tivoli in 1913. She developed into one of the clan of formidable women who reigned over Woods Road after she inherited Midwood. "Big Polly," as she was eventually known to distinguish her from her daughter with the same name, had the dimple gene but her sister Elizabeth was considered the great beauty of the family. Elizabeth married William Washburn, Frank's brother, adding symmetry to the family tree. Frank participated in only one endeavor on the grounds of Midwood—growing prized sweet peas under the protection of the property's greenhouses. The third sister, Mary, wed

PREVIOUS SPREAD Joan Davidson and her family enjoy breakfast in summer here under the umbrella on Midwood's lawn. LEFT The neo-Pompeian wall decorations are by Bill Hodgson. On the left is Horacio Torres's painting of Matt Davidson, and on the right, his brother, Brad. FOLLOWING SPREAD The portrait of Peter Davidson in the "piano room" was painted by Bruno Fonseca. A collection of books, published with Joan Davidson's assistance, sits in front of a fifteenth-century Peruvian tapestry.

John Gray and was responsible for selling Midwood following the death of her mother, Big Polly.

"Mary Gray left Midwood for the last time" was written on a Post-it note to greet Joan Davidson when she arrived at the house. In 1985 a Manhattan friend who owned a neighboring home on Woods Road informed Joan that Midwood had just come up for sale. Joan, who had no plans of acquiring a country house, arranged for a visit to satisfy her curiosity. Driving down Midwood's long, gracefully curving driveway, Joan remembers saying to herself, "Uh-oh, stay calm . . . never mind what the house will look like—it's the setting that matters!" She then discovered that she loved the house as well. After Mary Gray generously invited Joan, with friends and family, to "try out" the house for a weekend, Joan decided that she very much did want a country house after all; she immediately arranged for the purchase from the Grays, which included eighty-five acres and several ancillary buildings as well as many of the home's interior furnishings.

Soon thereafter Joan enlisted local architect Harry van Dyke (whose own Forth House she greatly admired) to analyze Midwood's condition and make whatever improvements might be needed. Together, they oversaw the removal of an unnecessary staircase, created a children's playroom, and doubled the size of the two living rooms. They also built a tower to add sleeping space as well as a studio. With landscape designer Eleanor M. McPeck, Joan strategically reframed the views of the Hudson River and beyond to the Catskill Mountains. A swimming pool was discreetly repositioned away from the house so as not to disturb the view from the porch.

Midwood is a rare property along the Hudson in that it includes acreage across the train tracks with direct access to the river. To punctuate this anomaly, Hart Perry and his wife, Dana, recently made a gift to Joan of a 100-year-old corncrib that had been part of the original farm fabric of their neighboring house, Southwood. The intention was to transport the bulky structure, "using ancient Egyptian ingenuity," in one piece, to serve as a boathouse. It traveled down a steep escarpment, over a bridge, to be positioned on the small one-acre parcel of land that projects into the Hudson River. This has become one of the prize landmarks on the river's shore, and the corncrib boathouse now stores kayaks, which the family often uses to explore the Hudson's coastline.

In 2015, Joan's son Matt and his wife, Amy, moved from Chicago to live in charming River House on the Midwood property. Matt has been president of the Open Space Institute, active in the family's J. M. Kaplan Fund, and president of several businesses, mostly in the Midwest. Upon landing back in New York, he was summoned by Rose Harvey, Commissioner of the New York State Office of Parks, Recreation and Historic Preservation, to take on the position of special assistant to the commissioner. His mother says, he is "expected to solve the unsolvable." Joan

---

PREVIOUS SPREAD Left: The mirror in the second-floor hall is the mate of the one hanging at Southwood. The bulletin board is filled with family photographs and artwork. Right: Various yard sale and flea-market purchases fill the sunlit kitchen. RIGHT The artist who painted the scenic walls in the bedroom remains a mystery. The dresser is a Livingston piece left by the home's previous owner, Mrs. Gray. A Federal sofa anchors the left side of the room.

LEFT The third-floor bedroom is referred to as "the dorm." ABOVE The "bamboo suite" takes its name from a group of eight pieces of bamboo-inspired furnishings from 1888. BELOW Camp Midwood T-shirts are displayed in the "map room."

had herself served as commissioner of state parks, in the 1990s; she was able to encourage the establishment of the Hudson River National Historic Landmark District.

The family's philanthropic reach was illustrated at Joan's ninetieth birthday celebration in 2017, held on the filled-to-capacity south lawn of the Cooper Hewitt, Smithsonian Design Museum. The list of recipients benefiting from grants made by the J. M. Kaplan Fund includes Carnegie Hall, the Westbeth Artists Community, and South Street Seaport in New York City. The fund's annual report publishes a paragraph from Joan that affirms its willingness ". . . to take chances so that fresh ideas in both the private and public realms can be safely tried out." An additional arm of the fund was established by Joan in 1995 to assist in the publication of nonfiction illustrated and printed books.

Midwood's annual Summer Shad party—a gathering of friends, family, and foundation co-workers who congregate on the west lawn—celebrates the river and the bony fish that navigate upriver in springtime.

Camp Midwood continues during the summer months. There are now twelve grandchildren whose stories and drawings are displayed all over the house, but are arranged especially along the rim of an immense Victorian mirror on the second-floor landing, which is the posting spot for creative expressions, leaving just enough space for the upcoming fourth generation.

---

**ABOVE AND RIGHT** Midwood's landing offers rare direct access to the Hudson. The boathouse, which was originally Southwood's corncrib, houses the family's kayaks.

STAATSBURGH

1895

STAATSBURGH HAS OFTEN BEEN considered the model for Bellomont, Gus and Judy Trenor's estate in Edith Wharton's 1905 novel *The House of Mirth*. Speculative as this might appear—there are no written references by Wharton stating this to be the case— several key passages and characters in the novel lead the way to this conclusion. The depiction of Bellomont as a house that enveloped an earlier one is the most telling. Many of the physical details were thinly disguised so as to maintain the owners' privacy. Wharton's aunt Elizabeth Schermerhorn Jones lived near Ruth and Ogden Mills at Wyndclyffe in Rhinebeck and took her niece with her when she was invited to Staatsburgh. The two families had memberships at the Coaching Club in Newport and traveled in the same social circles. Lily Bart, Wharton's heroine, who was anxious about losing coveted assets while playing cards and vacillating between the expectation of marrying a wealthy husband and the psychological cost in doing so, could easily have been a guest at Staatsburgh. In contrast, Wharton depicted Judy Trenor as a woman with a profoundly disciplined social ambition. The same observation was often made of Ruth Livingston Mills, the châtelaine of Staatsburgh during the home's apotheosis. Ruth brought numerous generations of elevated social position to her marriage, while her husband, Ogden Mills, brought an estimated seventeen million dollars. Together they ascended the ranks of New York, Newport, Paris, and Hudson Valley society, reaching the penultimate step just below that of Caroline Astor.

Seven generations of lineage associated with the Staatsburgh site began in 1792 when Morgan Lewis, the third governor of New York State and son of Francis, a signer of the Declaration of Independence, purchased 324 acres from descendants of Samuel Staats. In 1701, Staats, with Dirck Van Der Burgh, bought a portion of the land from Captain Henry Pawling's widow south of Rhinebeck. By the 1760s, the area was called Staatsburgh commemorating the combination of the two landowners' family names.

In 1779, Morgan Lewis married Gertrude Livingston at Clermont, her childhood home. He was quartermaster general of the Northern Army after serving with General Gates in Saratoga during the Revolutionary War. Over the course of ten years, beginning in 1780 when their only daughter, Margaret, was born, Gertrude was gifted a 1,618-acre portion of land in Rhinebeck by her mother, Margaret Beekman Livingston. The tenant farmers who occupied the land supplied Gertrude with an independent income. The couple rented Grasmere from Gertrude's sister Janet Montgomery for nine years until they were able to secure land in Staatsburgh. Here they built a simple brick home, known as Staatsburgh House, with a hipped roof that supported a cupola. During the summers, the house also sheltered the twelve children of Margaret and her husband, Maturin Livingston, Sr. Through this marriage

---

**PREVIOUS SPREAD** The impressive dining room at Staatsburgh was created in the Louis XIV style in 1895. The pilasters are clad in Campan Vert marble and the upper portions of the walls are in Cipollino marble. **RIGHT** Stanford White artfully integrated an earlier Livingston home into a Beaux-Arts house. He diverted the eye away from the fact that the central block of the original house contained three floors by adding a monumental Ionic portico, bridging the incompatible proportions of the old structure and White's additions.

among cousins, Maturin, Sr., reintroduced the Livingston name back into this branch of the family. In the following years, Morgan Lewis held positions including attorney general of New York State, chief justice of the New York State Supreme Court, governor of New York, and state senator. He also was the grand master of the New York chapter of the Freemasons and president of the Order of the Cincinnati. Eight boxes of The Morgan Lewis Papers are now held at the New-York Historical Society, where he was president in 1835. His formidable accomplishments earned him enormous respect and placed him in the epicenter of New York's early history.

When they were not in Rhinebeck, Maturin, Sr., and Margaret lived the rest of the year in New York City where he had his

---

**PREVIOUS SPREAD** A portrait of Gladys Mills Phipps, who donated the house to New York State in 1938, hangs to the left in the Baroque-style entrance hall. **OPPOSITE** Seventeenth-century tapestries decorate the main oak staircase above the entrance hall. **ABOVE** The ancestral portraits in the hall include from left, Robert "The Judge" Livingston, his wife, Margaret Beekman, and their son Robert "The Chancellor" Livingston.

law practice. They hired architect Benjamin Latrobe to design Ellerslie for them in Rhinebeck in 1809. The elegant Regency home served the large brood well until Morgan Lewis suffered a health crisis in 1814. Gertrude convinced her only child to move back to Staatsburgh with the family to help take care of him. This blatantly manipulative request was softened when two lateral wings were added to the original structure shortly thereafter, allowing more freedom of movement in the house for all three generations.

Joseph Bonaparte, the former king of Italy and Spain and Napoleon's brother, was a frequent guest. On Morgan Lewis's invitation Joseph toured the Hudson Valley looking for a suitable location to settle. Although he eventually situated himself in Bordentown, New Jersey, he visited Lewis annually. In 1824, the Marquis de Lafayette added his name to the list of illustrious guests when he stopped en route to stay at New Clermont.

In 1832, Staatsburgh House burned to the ground while the family members were at their winter home in Manhattan at 72 Leonard Street. It was immediately rebuilt by 1835 in the Greek Revival style, just in time for Louis Napoleon Bonaparte's visit. The dominant elements of the new house, simply called Staatsburgh, were the two-story porches, each with four Doric columns, on the

east and west elevations. The entablatures over the columns were composed of metopes decorated with diamond-shaped bosses. Julia Delafield, Margaret's daughter, wrote in her 1877 *Biography of Franois Lewis and Morgan Lewis* that the plan for the house had been drawn by her mother. The two bowed walls on the west elevation are still visible, and were incorporated into the enlarged house later designed by architect Stanford White.

In the mid-nineteenth century Margaret maintained the property after her parents and husband died. She was called "Grandma Grundy" by her grandchildren imitating the character committed to propriety in Thomas Morton's 1798 play *Speed the Plough*. In 1854, she gave thirty acres to her youngest daughter, Geraldine, upon her marriage to Lydig Hoyt, following the matriarchical tradition of the family. The Point was soon built on this stunning site by Calvert Vaux for the Hoyts.

Maturin Livingston, Jr., inherited Staatsburgh in 1860 following the death of his mother with the stipulation that he contribute 40,000 dollars within six months to be put into a trust. The property was not lucrative and she wanted to ensure that it was capable of remaining in the family despite its unprofitability.

His sister Julia married General Joseph Delafield. She was known in the family for an article she had written in 1857, but not published until 1877. Titled "The Upper Ten," she condescendingly addressed subjects as diverse as the nouveaux riches, and what makes one an aristocrat by birth. Her son Maturin Delafield inherited Montgomery Place from his cousin Coralie Barton and passed it on to his grandson John Ross Delafield in 1921.

When they received ownership of Staatsburgh, Maturin, Jr., and his wife, Ruth, moved in with their five-year-old identical twins, Ruth and Elizabeth. The girls entered society during a period of extreme excess. Maturin, Jr., was part of a privileged stratum of society that eventually formed the Patriarchs, a social club composed of twenty-five gentlemen from the strictest edit of influential families in New York City.

Ward McAllister, New York's social arbiter at that time, visited Staatsburgh, which he erroneously referred to as "Livingston Manor," when the twins were young girls. He stated, "All my life I had been taught to have a sort of reverence for the name of Livingston, and to feel that Livingston Manor was a species of palatial residence, that one must see certainly once in one's lifetime . . . Instead of a palace I found a fine, old fashioned country-house . . . At eleven every morning we were all in the saddle, and went off for a ride of some twenty miles, lunching at some fine house or another. It was English life to perfection, and most enjoyable."

In 1880, Elizabeth married William George Cavendish-Bentinck, a British peer and member of Parliament. Thoroughly trained in the arts of a châtelaine, she entered English society as the doyenne of Highcliffe Castle in Hampshire. She attended the coronation of King Edward VII and was a crucial social sponsor for wealthy Americans visiting England.

---

Her sister, Ruth, wed Ogden Mills in 1882, forming an unsurpassed alliance. Ogden's father was Darius Ogden Mills, whose vast fortune had started with selling pickaxes and shovels during the California Gold Rush of 1049. Not interested in panning for gold, he began a business providing fellow enthusiasts with the supplies and tools needed to reap the best rewards. Within a year, he had 40,000 dollars in his pocket. In 1850, he started the D. O. Mills Bank, and at age twenty-five he became California's most powerful banker. Mills purchased 1,500 acres in San Mateo County, just north of today's Silicon Valley and humbly named the area Millbrae. The home he built, called Happy House, is still standing and was decorated by Herter Brothers, the famous Gilded Age design firm. Mills became the first president and co-founder in 1864 of the Bank of California, even loaning the bank one million dollars of his own money during a rough patch. Between 1870 and 1882, he was a director of Wells Fargo and Company. Unbeknownst to him, his son's future neighbor, Johnston Livingston of Callendar House, had held the same position after founding the company in 1852.

In 1881, Darius's daughter, Elisabeth, married Whitelaw Reid, editor of the *New York Tribune*, and Darius moved back to New York to continue his financial and social ascent. He constructed the Mills Building at 15 Broad Street at a cost of three million dollars, making it the most expensive privately owned office building in Manhattan. Following the trajectory of the period, he achieved the position of New York titan by serving as the president of the New York Botanical Garden and board member of The Metropolitan Museum of Art. His townhouse was at 634 Fifth Avenue, opposite St. Patrick's Cathedral, then considered the most fashionable locale in Manhattan. The bill he received after giving the Herter Brothers interior decorating firm carte blanche approached 450,000 dollars, which "disturbed his serenity," noted his friend the financier Henry Clews in 1888.

Darius's son, Ogden, evidently grew up in splendor. After attending Harvard University, he eased his way into the family businesses, but never made the spectacular impression his father had and remained somewhat in his shadow.

The other participant in the American marriage of the century, which occured in 1882, was Ruth Livingston. Following a blueprint of her own, Ruth felt assured of her dominance in a newly expanding society. The problem was that Caroline Astor had no intentions of vacating her throne. The social roar of this diminutive woman, known as "Tiny," became well documented, not least through Wharton's characterization of Judy Trenor. Following their marriage, the couple began construction of a Venetian Gothic–style townhouse designed by Richard Morris Hunt at 2 East Sixty-ninth Street. The boldly innovative neo-Louis XV and XVI rooms were furnished by Allard et Fils, which had opened a New York outpost for its Paris firm in 1885.

In 1890, Ward McAllister published *Society as I Have Found It* in which he unwittingly painted himself and the Patriarchs as a superficial and foolish group. The public tide of opinion about New York's upper crust had turned and, in 1892, McAllister finally published his list of "The Four Hundred," ironically signaling society's decline. The same year Mrs. Astor's husband died, followed by the death of her daughter and subsequent scandal caused by another daughter's marital infidelity, offering a trifecta of reasons to seclude herself. During this time a vacuum was created that Ruth was strategically poised to fill. Her exclusivity would not serve her well, however. Society and the public found the cult of rudeness she perpetuated, which had worked so well for Mrs. Astor twenty years prior, *démodé* and uncivil. The Patriarchs disbanded in 1897, the aging Mrs. Astor passed away in 1908, and her townhouse was finally demolished in 1939.

Ruth inherited Staatsburgh in 1890 following the death of her father, Maturin, Jr., in 1888, as it seems that her mother didn't want the responsibility. That year the town removed the "h" from the end of its name as part of a nationwide simplification project. Ruth and Ogden spent several autumns there before contemplating any changes. The house gave a tacit social advantage to Ruth, still intent on maintaining an unimpeachable social position. The fact that it was an actual ancestral estate distinguished it from the newly minted mansions being constructed by the upcoming generation of Industrial Age millionaires often documented by Wharton.

What the "old-fashioned country house" mentioned by McAllister missed was the impressive scale needed to remain competitive with the new breed of Beaux-Arts "cottages" being erected from which she could wage her campaign for social dominance.

Stanford White was completing Madison Square Garden when the Millses contracted with him to start work on their home in Dutchess County. White researched British country houses extensively before proposing a design to the Millses. Claremount House

**ABOVE** The bronze mantel clock was purchased by Allard et Fils, who decorated the house at the turn of the century. **OPPOSITE** Narcissus and Echo are the subjects of the seventeenth-century tapestry in the dining room.

in Surrey offered inspiration for this project, as did the work of architect James Gibbs. Closely studied was the White House in Washington, D.C., designed by Irish architect James Hoban, as well as its porticos, which were designed by Benjamin Latrobe.

Indeed, the parallels drawn with the White House were not by coincidence. The width of the east facade is identical at 170 feet and the depth is 6 feet shorter. Stanford White used the width of the original house to dictate the scale of the new massive Roman Ionic portico. White also referenced the Virginia State Capitol, designed by Thomas Jefferson in 1797. Two extremely large wings housing the dining room and the library were added to the original house on the north and south sides, each measuring fifty feet long by thirty feet wide with eighteen-foot ceilings. The cubic mass of each of these rooms is an imposing 27,000 square feet.

The interiors were furnished with an elevated Gilded Age vocabulary. The entrance was paneled in the English Baroque style, but what set this room apart from its rivals was that Ruth hung legitimate ancestral portraits on the walls as a tangible manifestation of her heritage, while her contemporaries were purchasing unidentified portraits in Europe that added only an artificial note of gravitas to their homes.

The imposing splendor of the dining room incorporated the dado, pilasters, and fireplace, which were made of Campan Vert marble, the same stone used in the Grand Appartement du Roi at Versailles. Flemish verdure tapestries were installed between panels of white Cipollino marble on the upper portions of the walls, adding the subtlest suggestion of warmth. This room was designed to overwhelm even the most cultivated and seasoned guest.

Allard et Fils was employed to furnish most of the principal rooms in the house under Stanford White's supervision. Correspondence of White to the Millses suggests shopping resources while they traveled in Europe, as there were sixty-five rooms and fourteen bathrooms to furnish. Twenty-four servants were employed while the family was in residence. The double parlor from the original house was adapted to become the green sitting room, keeping the original mantels as homage to the earlier structure. The Millses arrived to stay for the first time in their completed home in May 1896, nonplussed by the 350,000 dollars bill from Stanford White's office awaiting them.

Frederick and Louise Vanderbilt visited the Millses in 1895 to observe the progress on their friends' house. Ogden took them on a carriage ride to Hyde Park, a neighboring estate downriver recently placed for sale by the heirs of Walter Langdon, Jr. Fifty years earlier the property had been a gift to his mother from his grandfather John Jacob Astor. The Vanderbilts took the bait and immediately commissioned McKim, Mead & White to up the ante on the Hudson River.

Tradition held that the family spent summer in Newport, decamping to Staatsburgh from autumn until Christmas, when Ogden's ripe cantaloupes would be served from his heated greenhouses. The family then moved to New York with their twin daughters, Beatrice and Gladys, as well as their son, Ogden Livingston Mills. A side trip was taken to London in 1905 so that the Misses Millses could be presented at Buckingham Palace before Edward VII and Queen Alexandra. Beatrice married Edward's Lord-in-Waiting and Master of the Horse, the Eighth Earl of Granard, in 1909 in the ballroom of the Millses's townhouse in New York, becoming the Countess Granard. Her sister, Gladys, married Henry

Carnegie Phipps in 1907 at Staatsburgh, and Ogden Livingston Mills married Margaret Stuyvesant Rutherfurd in 1911 at the bride's château in Deauville, France. After 1914, spring was spent in Paris at their eighteenth-century Hôtel de Broglie located at 73 Rue de Varenne. Ruth died in 1920, Ogden in 1929, right before the devastating stock market crash. He had gone on a shopping spree in the 1920s, buying up neighboring farms, so that when he passed away, the size of the property had increased to include 1,608 acres. In 1918, he named the agricultural business Endekill Farm.

When the Millses were in residence at Staatsburgh during the fall season, golf, tennis, and horseback riding were offered to their guests. The family's horses, which were boarded at Wheatley Stable on Long Island, were brought to Staatsburgh just for the season. Legendary games of bridge that were part of the weekend schedule often lasted past midnight. In fact, these games are referenced in Edith Wharton's *The House of Mirth*: they are yet another literary clue that identifies Bellomont as Staatsburgh.

In 1926, Ogden Livingston Mills, then secretary of the treasury under Herbert Hoover, and his sister Gladys started a second Wheatley Stable, based at Claiborne Farm in Paris, Kentucky. Their mares produced Bold Ruler, sire to Secretariat, and Sea Biscuit, among other famous racehorses.

---

**ABOVE** A corner of the library containing many generations of books collected by the family. **RIGHT** General Morgan Lewis's portrait is positioned over the mantel in the parcel-gilt oak library, which was the gathering place after dinner for card games.

LEFT Ruth Livingston Mills's bedroom is upholstered in fabric reproduced by Scalamandré. **ABOVE AND BELOW** The bedroom of Ogden Mills was en suite with that of his wife, connected, with their shared marble bath.

The last year the house was inhabited was 1934. Ogden died at the age of fifty-three while at his parents' home at 2 East Sixty-ninth Street. In 1937, Gladys was living in Wesbury, Long Island, at her home, Spring Hill when she deeded Staatsburgh with 192 acres to New York State. Her daughter Audrey Phipps Holden recently explained that "it was considered by this generation to be in extremely bad taste to live so conspicuously," further describing the shifting sentiments following the Great Depression. Later, in 1970, she gifted the contents of the house's interior to the New York State Office of Parks, Recreation and Historic Preservation.

Pam Malcolm, the Historic Site Manager of Staatsburgh State Historic Site, is tasked with implementing maintenance and repairs that were already long overdue when Gladys gifted the house in the 1930s. Stanford White had not understood that the construction and materials he chose were not appropriate for this windswept location and the destruction from this oversight was visible early on. Unfortunately, in 1957, the house was coated with sprayed-on Gunite to cover cracks obscuring White's details and ornamentation. Pam has overseen restoration of the front gates and Ruth Mills's bedroom and has spearheaded a three-million-dollar renovation of the front portico in 2013. Going forward, plans are in place to restore the upholstery, and analyze the remaining facades.

The family that resided at Staatsburgh for five generations is no longer present, but the ethos of the culture lives on in Wharton's work, which illustrates her complex and enduring relationship with the Hudson Valley.

---

**ABOVE** The servants used the back staircase, which also gave access to the maid's quarters in the attic. **OPPOSITE** Outside the dining room, the butler's pantry housed the family's collection of silver and porcelain. **FOLLOWING SPREAD** Viewed from Staatsburgh's roof, the dramatic sunset over the Hudson River is reminiscent of the nineteenth-century paintings by Frederic Edwin Church.

# FOXHOLLOW FARM
## 1910

THOMAS WOLFE OFFERS A DESCRIPTION of the view from Foxhollow Farm in his 1935 novel *Of Time and the River* that encapsulates his impressions of the region: " . . . the fragrance of the night came in slowly, sustaining gauzy curtains on its breath of coolness like a cloud of gossamer . . . in the distance the great wink and scallop-dance and dark unceasing mystery of the lovely and immortal river—a landscape such as one might see in dreams . . ."

Wolfe had befriended Olin Dows while the two were at Harvard College and had stayed often in Rhinebeck at Foxhollow Farm, the house Olin's parents, Alice and Tracy Dows, had commissioned from architect Harrie T. Lindeberg in 1906. In his book, Wolfe painted a detailed portrait of the Dows family, whom he had renamed the Pierces, and the house and property, which he called Far Field Farm. The Dowses later offered him the Gate Lodge, also designed by Lindeberg, so that he could have a quiet place to work on *Look Homeward, Angel*. Located at the southern border of the estate, where the Landsman Kill empties into Vanderburgh Cove on its way to the Hudson River, the Gate Lodge effectively communicates an invitation and anticipates the well-expressed Colonial Revival design of the main house up the hill. Wolfe wrote of the location, as " . . . a little bit of heaven with a little river, a wooded glade, and the sound of water falling over the dam all through the night."

Olin became Joel Pierce in the story that delved deeply into the social milieu Wolfe found so captivating. He referred to the people he met as "Swells . . . of a colony for millionaires, a very old Dutch place, called Rhinebeck. His people are fabulously wealthy—as wealthy or wealthier than the Asheville Vanderbilts . . ." Rhinebeck became thinly and ineffectively veiled as Rhinekill.

Foxhollow Farm was built on the site of Linwood Hill, an 1841 villa designed by architect A. J. Davis for Dr. Federal Vanderburgh. John Barber James and his wife, Mary Vanderburgh, had purchased Linwood Hill in 1849 from her father, who moved into neighboring Linwood, the eighteenth-century house of Alice's ancestor, Dr. Thomas Tillotson. Henry James spent many summers with his aunt and uncle, John and Mary James, and reflected on his time there in his 1913 book *A Small Boy and Others* " . . . Didn't Lin-

wood bristle with great views and other glories, with the gardens and graperies, and black ponies, to say nothing of gardeners and grooms who were notoriously and quotedly droll."

Alice Olin Dows was born in 1881. Her mother, Elsie, tragically died soon after giving birth to her sister, Julia, when Alice was only a year and a half old. They were raised at her maternal grandparents home at 1 Madison Avenue, which contained an important collection of old master paintings. The sisters spent summers at Glenburn, their father's ancestral home in Rhinebeck, which Alice had romanticized as the most beautiful spot on earth as a young girl. Predictably, she married married Tracy Dows there in 1903. Ruth Livingston Mills, a distant relative, supplied the wedding flowers and provided the dock at her home Staatsburgh from which they left for their honeymoon on Tracy's yacht, the *Mohican*.

Following their marriage, Alice and Tracy lived across the street from Ogden and Ruth Livingston Mills on the top floor of the townhouse at 1 East Sixty-ninth Street in Manhattan built by Tracy's father, David Dows, using the fortune he accumulated trading grain and commodities. Anxious to get out from under her mother-in-law's critical gaze, the young couple moved to Woodland Cottage in Irvington, where Alice had her first two children—Olin, in 1904, and Margaret, in 1906.

During a visit in 1905, when Alice and Tracy were visiting her father, Stephen Henry Olin, at Glenburn, he informed the newlyweds that neighboring Linwood Hill was going to become available for sale from local farmer George Holliday. On this plateau of land with its magnificent views of the Hudson and beyond, the Dowses became intoxicated and envisioned their new home.

Foxhollow Farm's architect, Harrie T. Lindeberg, opened his practice with Lewis Colt Albro in 1906. Lindeberg, who had been Stanford White's personal assistant, had worked on the townhouse of Charles Dana Gibson at 127 East Seventy-third Street, and it was Gibson who recommended Lindeberg to his good friends the Dowses before leaving the office of McKim, Mead & White. Lindeberg's second wife, Lucia Hull, was a Livingston descendant and distantly related to Alice Dows. Alice had known Stanford White since she was a young girl living near Gramercy Park, where her father had developed a friendship with him at The Players social club and often entertained him at their home. The first building to be completed at Foxhollow Farm, in 1907, was the Stone Cottage, later the farm superintendent's house, which the Dows family moved into while the main house was being built. This was to become the home rented by Madge Telfair, the character based on Alice's distant cousin Laura Delano, in *Of Time and the River*. Laura rented the cottage while John Russell Pope was working on Evergreen Lands, her new home near Foxhollow Farm.

At the dawn of the twentieth century, there was a reaction to the excesses of the end of the nineteenth century, with its weighted

**PREVIOUS SPREAD** Harrie T. Lindeberg designed the colonnaded front of the house with reference to Mount Vernon, as one of his commissions after leaving McKim, Mead & White. **LEFT** Olin Dows at age thirteen painting panels in the loggia that were later installed above a shop's entrance in Rhinebeck. **OPPOSITE** A photograph taken in 1916 of the the back terrace that was the family's favorite place to entertain and serve afternoon tea.

Victorian gloom. Originally thinking a brick Georgian house would convey an attractive gravitas, the Dowses subsequently requested a home that referenced Mount Vernon, the Virginia estate of George Washington, and The Orchard, the home of James Breese in Southampton, also designed by Lindeberg. Eight Doric columns set on marble bases supporting a flat roof with a decorative balustrade became the dominant features on the east entrance elevation. Two projecting wings on the west facade contained the kitchen and the loggia, which became the most frequented work space for Olin when he began painting at a young age. Alice furnished the rest of the house with English antiques purchased at Vernay's in New York.

Edward Burnett and Alfred Hopkins conceived the barn complex at Foxhollow. The architects had worked together on George Wash-

ington Vanderbilt's property at the Biltmore Estate in Asheville, North Carolina. Within the walls of the estate are a classical children's playhouse with Doric columns, a coachmen's house, stables for horses and prized Brown Swiss cows, a pheasantry for Dows's ring-necked pheasants and partridges, and enough housing to shelter the forty servants needed to run the property.

Frederick Law Olmsted's sons established the successor firm Olmsted Brothers, and were hired to create a master plan that incorporated many of the neighboring farms absorbed by Dows into his landholding of 800 acres. Dows purchased 240 acres from the Crosbys, neighbors at Grasmere, creating a tract that spanned the triangle framed by the Fallsburg Creek, Landsman Kills, Vanderburgh Cove, and the Albany Post Road.

Every detail of the young family's domestic life was impeccably documented by Tracy Dows, who was rarely without his Graflex camera. Alice wrote, "Where he outdid himself was in photography. He was thoughtful and generous and loved to give people pleasure and when the impulse settled on Kodak pictures his friends and family might receive at least once a week a batch of a dozen prints." The massive collection of photographs taken over a thirty-year span and contained within twenty-two leather-bound volumes now resides at Hudson River Heritage in Rhinebeck and was recently incorporated into a comprehensive book by David Byars, *Our Time at Foxhollow Farm*.

In the fall of 1910, the family moved from Stone Cottage into the recently finished main house, Foxhollow Farm. Alice later described "a life of overwhelming leisure." Tracy immediately integrated himself into the community by becoming an investor in the Rhinebeck Realty Company, which relocated the Dutchess County Fair to its present site nearby. He became one of several investors who purchased the Rhinebeck Hotel in 1914. Originally named Traphagen Tavern, established in 1705, it was in great need of a facelift. In 1917, Lindeberg was again brought up to Dutchess County to transform the eighteenth-century building, "the oldest continuously open hotel in the country," into one with an updated classical facade reminiscent of the house at Foxhollow Farm. Tracy then renamed it The Beekman Arms Hotel in homage to his wife's lineage.

Over the next thirteen years, the Dows family often closed up the house in Rhinebeck and traveled with staff and tutors in tow. Several winters were spent in Paris at Helen and Vincent Astor's house in the Bois de Boulogne with Olin enrolled at L'Ecole des Beaux-Arts. Olin had previously studied with his cousin Robert Chanler and at the Art Students League. Olin told local author Cynthia Owen Philip, "God only knows how much growing up in a beautifully sited house of good design and with good furniture, surrounded by acres of well-kept lawns, fields, and woodlands affects one's perceptions." She added that he was acutely conscious that being privileged, and taking such an environment for granted permanently shaped his innermost being.

In 1924, Helen Astor gave Alice and Tracy's eldest daughter, Margaret, who had been a flower girl at her wedding, a dance at 840 Fifth Avenue, previously the home of her mother-in-law Caroline Astor, and now the site of Temple Emanu-El. The following year Margaret married Knut Richard Thyberg, a Swedish diplomat, and moved to Sweden, where Alice's first grandchild was born a year later. He was called "O. K.," for Olin Knut. In the 1920s, Alice's friend British painter Sir Oswald Birley, painted her portrait that was included in an exhibition at Duveen Brothers at 730 Fifth Avenue. She eventually received the cherished portrait as a gift from the artist.

By the mid-1920s, Alice and Tracy began to live separately. Tracy took up rooms at the Connaught in London and Alice moved to Washington, D.C., where she could indulge herself in the culture of the city. Olin decorated his mother's Georgetown house with murals depicting the enchanting landscape at Glenburn and Foxhollow Farm. Here, Alice published *Illusions*, her second volume of verse, and acquired an assortment of international friends. At the same time, Olin was receiving commissions to paint screens, panels, and murals for a cultivated clientele. Around 1930, while staying with Margaret in London, Alice visited Diana and Reed Vreeland at their flat in London to see the overmantel panel of cats Olin had painted for the Vreelands' daring chartreuse and scarlet dining room.

Following the financial crisis of 1929, Tracy decided that it would be best if the family were to leave the farm permanently. He commented that they had reduced the staff by this time, "to two in the house and two outdoors." He turned the house over to Aileen Farrell, who had been a tutor to their third child, Deborah. Farrell established the Foxhollow School there (she later relocated the school up the road to Grasmere and then to Lenox, Massachusetts). Olin and Alice moved back to Glenburn after Tracy unexpectedly died in 1937.

In 1938, Vincent Astor purchased Foxhollow Farm from the three children and lent it to his brother John Jacob Astor V for two years. Deborah "Deb" Dows kept 200 acres of what had been called Southlands, where the sheep pasture had been. In response to her mother's excessive lifestyle, Deb gravitated toward a simpler life outside of society. She soon established the Southlands Foundation, a riding facility that is still running strong today. The house she built on the property, Hog Hollow, was modeled on a farmhouse she had visited in Germany and was partially constructed using bricks she salvaged from the Rutsen Chapel on Vincent Astor's property. Foxhollow Farm went through several incarnations before finding its present occupant, Samaritan Daytop Village.

Alice befriended neighbor Gore Vidal, who was to remain close to her until her death in 1963. In typical fashion, Vidal wrote, "To the mystification of the Valley, Alice Dows and I were a sort of romantic couple until her death. I suppose it was assumed that I was some sort of gerontophile . . . She was buried in my letters."

*Of Time and the River* was finally published in 1935. Alice, the woman who had greeted Wolfe with the icy disdain reserved for those who had never dressed for dinner, was ". . . horrified that he dared to record our lives." She did reflect, however, "How many times since have I regretted the absurd waste of these days. And how much that I took as a matter of course and completely natural was definitely wrong. My ignorance was abysmal. I had a natural love of luxury. Tracy had been brought up to (as well), so between us it was fatal." Not entirely humbled, Alice was still capable of the occasional cutting remark, as when she whispered to Vidal at Edgewater, "Such a pity, the way Eleanor [Roosevelt] has let her figure go." Oddly, she never complained when forced to accept much reduced circumstances later in life.

Wolfe never finished his second novel set in the area, which he had given the working title *The River People*, but one can still appreciate Wolfe's observations when he first encountered the area. "And above all else, the Hudson River was like the light—Oh, more than anything, it was the light . . . that made the Hudson River wonderful." In following, he described Foxhollow Farm as ". . . a dream house, such as one sees only in a dream." The great white house still stands today, albeit in a compromised state. This important example of Lindeberg's early work awaits the next chapter that will return its former elegance.

---

The one-and-a-half-story stone Gate Lodge was designed in 1906 by Harrie T. Lindeberg as the entrance to Foxhollow Farm near South Mill Road in Rhinebeck. Thomas Wolfe spent time here in the 1920s while writing *Look Homeward, Angel*.

# MARIENRUH

## 1926

UPON HER MARRIAGE TO Prince Serge Obolensky in 1924, Alice Astor's brother, Vincent, gave her ninety-nine acres from the northern part of their ancestral country seat, Ferncliff, in Rhinebeck. Along with the land, he gifted Alice a set of diamond earrings once sewn into Marie-Antoinette's corsage while she was fleeing Paris before being brought to the Bastille. In 1912, twenty-year-old Vincent had been left the bulk of his father's vast estate, setting a high bar for the kind of gifts circulated in the family. Prince Paul of Serbia was the best man at Alice's wedding and Waldorf, Viscount Astor, Alice's second cousin from the English branch of the family, gave her away.

The tract of land included in Vincent's gift was referred to as Clifton Point, and had been purchased in 1868 by Louis Augustus Ehlers, Ferncliff's landscape designer, following his marriage to Mary Delamater. He built himself a wooden Italianate farmhouse with a wraparound porch that took advantage of the magical views of the Hudson River. Ehlers named the property Marienruh in homage to his wife, Mary—*ruh* meaning "rest" in German. Alice's

father, John Jacob Astor IV, purchased Ehler's home in 1900 and had it torn down two years before she was born.

Alice Astor, according to Gore Vidal, " . . . was slender . . . pale-skinned; from some angles she was beautiful. Alice inherited five million dollars from her father . . . after he perished on the *Titanic* in 1912. When she died, in 1956, she left exactly five million dollars in her estate, despite the extravagance of her husbands as well as generous gifts to all sorts of mysterious adventurers aprowl in the psychic world." The photographer Cecil Beaton captured her

PREVIOUS SPREAD Left: The Obolensky coat of arms is incorporated above the entrance of Marienruh. Right: Architect Mott B. Schmidt designed the Georgian-style house on land that was given to Alice Astor by her brother Vincent on the occasion of her marriage to Serge Obolensky. ABOVE The dependencies were designed with recessed arched windows. OPPOSITE The current renovation is focused on returning Marienruh to its former glory.

unusual features in his portrait from 1937 and again later while she was a guest at his house at Ashcombe in Wiltshire, England.

Alice's mother, Ava, divorced John Jacob Astor IV in 1909 out of boredom and married the dashing Baron Ribblesdale in 1919 after moving to London with Alice. Easily dissatisfied, Ava was overheard by Serge complaining, "Isn't life frightful?" with a devilish smile to cousin Nancy Astor upon leaving Cliveden, the home of the British branch of the Astor family, and stepping into her Rolls-Royce.

Alice and Serge were introduced at a golf foursome in 1922 by Baba Curzon, whose father Lord Curzon, had been Viceroy of India until 1905 and had sponsored the unveiling of King Tutankhamun's tomb, which Alice attended. Serge outwitted Ivo Churchill, son of the Duke and Duchess of Marlborough, for Alice's hand just before they attended the wedding of Baba and Edward "Fruity" Metcalf in 1925. After their honeymoon in Deauville, the Obolenskys returned to New York, where they stayed with Vincent at 840 Fifth Avenue. Vincent then transported the Obolenskys to Beechwood, the Astor's Newport house, and finally up the Hudson to Ferncliff in his boat, the *Nourmahal*, which he had financed with his profits from the film *Ben-Hur*. The couple's son, Ivan, was born in 1925, and their daughter, Sylvia, in 1931.

The Obolenskys were working with architect Mott B. Schmidt in 1925 to design Marienruh, a five-part Georgian-style stone house with thirty rooms. The site they chose was away from the Hudson so as to avoid the soot emanating from the passing trains. Schmidt's inspiration for Marienruh came from the eighteenth-century Hammond-Harwood House and Montpelier, both in Maryland. The original request was for a Queen Anne-style manor, but Schmidt, who was heavily influenced by the wave of scholarly interest in early colonial architecture in the 1920s, persuaded them to keep an open mind to his new aesthetic. Once the final plans were drawn up, the Obolenskys chose to name the house Marienruh in recognition of the previous home on the property. Contained in the pediment of the central pavilion is an oculus above the carved stone Obolensky crest, which is positioned on top of Marienruh's front door. Schmidt had received his big break in 1920 when literary agent Elizabeth Marbury and her girlfriend, interior decorator Elsie de Wolfe, hired him to design their home on Sutton Place. Marbury was an integral part of the social fabric of the period, and around that time, she introduced Schmidt to Vincent Astor, for whom he built an elegant Adam-style townhouse at 130 East Eightieth Street

The Obolensky's new residence was filled with exquisite furnishings brought from Hanover Lodge, the couple's London home, along with numerous early nineteenth-century Russian portraits by Vladimir Borovikovsky. Their son, Ivan, rode Cleopatra, his Egyptian racing donkey, and loved to jump onto his Uncle Vincent's miniature steam railway, which ran in a loop around Ferncliff.

The home swelled with the creative intelligentsia whom Alice was fond of hosting. After spending time with Rudyard Kipling discussing the afterlife, Alice believed she had been reincarnated from Queen Tiye of Pharaonic Egypt. Gore Vidal recalled in his autobiography, *Palimpsest*, that "She had also come into the possession of the queen's necklace which looked cursed to anyone like me, who had been brought up on the film *The Mummy*. At Rhinecliff she lived as if she were still English."

Squeaky Hatch tells of the evening that another eccentric brother and sister, writers Osbert and Edith Sitwell, were being entertained at Marienruh. Alice had invited Kate Osborn, of Callendar House, " . . . to help in case of friction. To everyone's relief, Vincent and the Sitwells got along famously, even entering a friendly contest about who had been the most badly treated as a child by their parents. The chemistry was so good that Vincent offered to fly the Sitwells to New York City in his seaplane. Edith Sitwell had never flown before and was terrified, but as Kate said, 'with true British thrift she could not resist a free trip.'"

Serge Obolensky traced his roots back to the year 862 through Rurik, Grand Duke of Novgorod and Kiev. As one of the White Russians who had escaped the Revolution, he landed in Rome, and then moved to London, where he roomed with his cousin Prince Felix Yusupov, Rasputin's assassin. While in London, Serge was briefly engaged to "the terribly attractive" Standard Oil heiress Millicent Rogers, whom he described as "an exotic creature with a curious, languid manner." He met Alice after his previous marriage to Princess Catharine Bariatinsky in Russia had ended.

Alice undertook considerable research to establish, to her own satisfaction, that the Astors had once been butchers in Walldorf, Germany, and she thought this a nice antidote to the snobbism of her grandmother Caroline Astor. Brilliantly educated with knowledge of Hindu and Egyptian philosophy, Alice preferred more raffish—not to mention, more provocative—company. After Alice and Serge divorced in 1932, she married, in succession, Raimund von Hofmannsthal, with whom she had a daughter, Romana, and Philip Harding, with whom she had Emily, finally settling down with fourth husband, British architect David Pleydell-Bouverie, who designed the Astor Tea House on the Ferncliff property. Serge had moved into an apartment on Fifty-seventh Street with friends Gary Cooper and Bert Taylor, president of the New York

Stock Exchange. During the summers he lived in the Duke Box, Angier Biddle Duke's refitted stables in Southampton, which he shared with a bevy of eligible bachelors.

Despite no longer being married to Alice, Serge continued his friendship with Vincent. In 1935, Vincent received ownership of the St. Regis Hotel, which had been built by his father in 1904. Acknowledging Serge's unmatched social flair, Vincent brought him on board to invigorate the hotel. The Maxfield Parrish mural *Old King Cole*, commissioned by John Jacob Astor for the Knickerbocker Hotel, was installed in the now famous bar bearing the same name at the St. Regis. Obolensky opened the Maisonette Russe in the basement of the hotel, which soon became the epicenter of social life in New York City. To everyone's amazement, Czar Nicholas's chef from Livadia Palace was hired to prepare shish kabobs served on flaming swords.

In 1945, Serge received a request from the Plaza Hotel to help with some updating. After thumbing through his black book, he called Cecil Beaton to redecorate several suites. In 1949 he moved onto the Sherry-Netherland Hotel, where he hired Elsie de Wolfe, now Lady Mendl, to do the same.

Between 1956, when Alice died, and 1980, Marienruh went through several commercial iterations before being sold to Werner Valeur-Jensen for 300,000 dollars. "Valeur," as the property became known, once again opened as a commercial space used for conference rentals.

Present owners Andrew Solomon and his husband, John Habich Solomon, chanced upon the home in 2006 while they were looking at real estate in the area. "We were looking for a Hudson Valley house with authentic character. It was a dream come true. We first visited in the summer. It was overgrown and the rolling open landscape was neglected, but there was a sense of proportion, which was elegant." Solomon, a writer, continues, "We lived in the house for a couple of years in a patchwork kind of way, then Robert came on board . . ." With respect for the previous owners' name for the property, they have once again reinstated Marienruh as the name for their new home.

Interior designer Robert Couturier had already worked on the couple's West Village home, and is now assisting on Marienruh's interiors. The goal is to preserve the elegant austerity of the house while making the commodious space welcoming. "It is a house which was a throwback to another era. I like the sense of history even if it has a mantle of modernity wrapped around its shoulders. Schmidt's design has an enormous sense of dignity," noted Solomon. Their renovation plan largely reflects Schmidt's floor plan, and the perfectly proportioned rooms. However, the west pavilion is being transformed into a two-story library for Solomon's vast collection of books.

George, the couple's eight-year-old son, is eager to finally be living in the house after spending the duration of the renovation in a nearby rental. Joining him will be family members Blaine Solomon and Lucy and Oliver Scher, echoing the similarly untraditional structure of Alice Astor's family almost a century ago.

---

An elliptical reflecting pool was recently commissioned by owners Andrew Solomon and John Habich Solomon as part of their comprehensive plans for the restoration of the grounds.

ORLOT
1941

IT TAKES CLOSE TO FIVE MINUTES to travel the one-mile drive that leads up to Orlot without disturbing the dust and pebbles lining the path, which is why upon arriving one day, I was surprised to be greeted by Evelyn "Evie" Chanler with a lovely "Good afternoon," closely followed by, "Will you be needing more than ten minutes to photograph the house?"

Orlot represents the waning of the Livingston fortune, albeit in a dwelling filled with treasures assembled from a direct line of family members. The enigmatic name of the property is derived from the discovery of a reddish shale containing low-grade iron ore on the grounds many years ago. The ore was pulverized and mixed with milk to form a red pigment, which was used as a wash for barns in the region.

The present house was designed on 250 acres by Louis Bancel La Farge in 1939 for Lewis Stuyvesant "Stuyve" Chanler, who changed the name of the property from the Ore Lot farm to the more easily pronounced Orlot. Building a house during World War II proved challenging, as materials were difficult to come by, but Orlot was finally inhabited by 1942.

Orlot came into the family when John Winthrop Chanler purchased Chamberlain Farm and Ravenswood, another farm, in 1877 with the intention of establishing his own home on this combined land. Through a quick succession of deaths that included John's

wife, Margaret Astor Ward Chanler, and William Backhouse Astor, Sr., his ten children inherited Rokeby from their grandparents, leaving him somewhat embarassed at being a guest in their home. The property he had purchased nearby was meant to provide him independence and dignity—unfortunately he died that same year. John left the land to his son John "Archie" Armstrong Chanler, who in turn offered it to his brother Lewis Stuyvesant Chanler in 1924.

In 1921 Lewis had married his second wife, Julia Olin, who had spent summers at nearby Glenburn with her sister, Alice Olin Dows. The couple had meet at Tuxedo Park, New York. Following their marriage, Lewis and Julia moved to Rue de Grenelle in Paris, and traveled throughout Europe with Julia's best friend Elsie de Wolfe, Lady Mendl. Since they had no need for a country house, the couple refused the offer from Archie, who was at this time visiting them in Paris. Archie impulsively threatened to jump out of their win-

---

**PREVIOUS SPREAD** *Sky Girl*, Robert Chanler's magnificent folding screen painted in 1922, stands in the living room at Orlot behind Chanler family photographs. **ABOVE** A painting by Bradi Barth hangs in the bedroom hallway. **OPPOSITE** Orlot was built in 1941 by Lewis Stuyvesant Chanler, Jr., on land entailed in the early 1920s to his young son Bronson "Bim" Chanler.

ABOVE Rhinebeck artist Olin Dows painted the 1915 lacquered panel of cranes on the left in the dining room. BELOW In 1928 artist A. K. Lawrence painted the Chanlers while in England.

dow if the offer was not accepted before realizing that their sister, Margaret, who now resided at their family home, Rokeby, would not take well to a divorced couple living nearby. Quickly switching gears, Archie gifted the property to his great nephew Bronson "Bim" Winthrop Chanler who was a young child. Therefore Bim's father, Lewis Stuyvesant Chanler, Jr., as guardian, built the present home where Bim was raised by his parents.

Bim's step-grandmother Julia Olin Chanler, who returned to New York in the late 1920s, became involved with the writings of Bahá'u'lláh and Abdu'l-Bahá and their teachings at the Bahá'í Center in New York City. While at the center, she organized talks at the Center by Albert Einstein, Rabindranath Tagore, Ilya Tolstoy, and the Grand Duke Alexander of Russia. Julia wrote of her husband Lewis "He was the portrait of an old master, brought to life under modern conditions and living with the freedom and detachment of a visitor to our times." His law practice consisted mainly of providing pro bono services to clients unable to afford counsel. Upon his death in 1942, the *Poughkeepsie New Yorker* wrote, ". . . Lewis Stuyvesant Chanler, Sr., last survivor of Dutchess County's famous Democratic dynasty of Chanler brothers who made history in the first dozen years of this century died of a heart ailment at his home, 132 East Sixty-fifth Street, New York."

Evie Chanler has occupied the house since her father-in-law, Lewis Stuyvesant Chanler, Jr.'s, death in 1963. Evie's son, who introduces himself with his weighty full name, John Armstrong Livingston Chanler, oversees the property. He was named in honor of his father's great-uncle John, or "Archie." His father, Bim, who died in 2009, had been the captain of the Harvard crew team before becoming an investment counselor at Train and Cabot in Manhattan. During weekends in Red Hook, Bim drove a jeep with a dented front fender, purposefully damaged by a ball bearing

that had been released from a slingshot by his eccentric cousin Chanler Chapman after a visit to Sylvania, Chapman's home. Bim's mother, Leslie Chanler, often contributed to Chapman's paper the *Barrytown Explorer* under the nom de plume "Country Cousin" while living at Orlot.

When Bim took possesion of Orlot, many family pieces were already in the home, including artworks by his great uncle Robert Chanler and cousin Olin Dows. The property is now separated from its neighbor Steen Valetje by a county road leading to the Kingston-Rhinecliff Bridge. The original 1770 house on the former Chamberlain Farm is still located along the private unpaved approach to Orlot. This road once provided access to Schultz's Landing, the crossing point of the Hudson River. Following a full day's visit, which necessitated longer than my "allotted" ten minutes, I drove away with the sense that there is a strong vein of history running through Orlot.

**ABOVE** English artist Albert Sterner painted the portrait of Lieutenant Governor of New York State Lewis Stuyvesant Chanler that hangs in the entrance hall above the family porcelain.
**FOLLOWING SPREAD** Various family treasures are assembled in the living room under the tray ceiling.

# ASTOR TEA HOUSE

## 1946

MARY "MINNIE" CUSHING CREATED some havoc during her tenure as Livingston descendent Vincent Astor's second wife. After insisting in the 1940s that her husband tear down his family's ancestral home, Ferncliff in Rhinebeck, because it reminded her of his previous wife, a fissure developed in the marriage. When things proved intolerable between the couple, Minnie secluded herself in what the family referred to as The Tea House, before divorcing Astor in 1953. As the eldest of the three fabulous Cushing sisters, her breeding encouraged the securing of a highly advantageous union. Her middle sister, Betsy, married President Franklin Delano Roosevelt's son James, and then John Hay Whitney. Her younger sister, Barbara, or "Babe," first married Stanley Mortimer of Standard Oil, then William Paley, founder and chairman of CBS.

The Tea House stands near the footprint of old Ferncliff and is north of the Stanford White–designed Casino, where the couple had been living. Visitors drove past Ferncliff Lodge and proceeded down what present owner Robert Duffy, founder and deputy chairman of Marc Jacobs International, has named Tea House Lane. The Tea House was designed during Vincent and Minnie's marriage by David Pleydell-Bouverie, the British architect who was Vincent's brother-in-law. Centered on Astor Cove, it strategically occupied pride of place on the plateau overlooking the Hudson River. Archival photographs show a charming small brick octagonal folly with lateral pendants on the north and south. The Tea House was a loose interpretation of Richard Mique's 1781 Belvedere Pavilion at Versailles.

The home that Duffy purchased had in the interim undergone an unsympathetic enlargement that begged for a major overhaul. "The core of the folly was enchanting, but the exterior was clad in a mock stucco finish," remembers interior designer Richard McGeehan, who has collaborated with Duffy on nine previous projects. McGeehan was brought on board to introduce a spirit within the walls that reflected his client's eclectic collections and enthusiastic but unorthodox aesthetic. McGeehan remembers his first visit to the house: "The obvious magic of being on a hill overlooking the Hudson River; the living room literally hangs on a cliff, sealed the deal for Robert." The slumbering landscape was overgrown, obscuring the view at the time but sheltering many vestiges of the Astor family. Duffy repaired the stone wall that borders the property on River Road, and with his daughter Victoria, age six, continues "to discover architectural remnants and garden features left on the property after Ferncliff was intentionally imploded."

PREVIOUS SPREAD A pair of Foo dogs guard the Astor Tea House's back lawn terrace. Originally a rustic roadway, this area was part of a system of carriage drives within the Ferncliff estate. OPPOSITE The large Bohemian chandelier in the entrance hall previously hung in the living room in the 1940s. Unusual angled hallways surround the octagonal structure. ABOVE Four nineteenth-century iron columns, from Vauxhall, London, were left in their original condition.

PREVIOUS SPREAD The living room—a thirty-foot octagonal space with six sets of French doors that lead to every part of the house—is the core of the original Tea House. The room is an eclectic mix of periods reflecting present owner Robert Duffy's travels. OPPOSITE The small private library that opens into the master bedroom was referred to in David Pleydell-Bouverie's plan as Mrs. Astor's watercolor studio. The marble fireplace mantel is said to have come from Ferncliff. ABOVE The master bedroom includes Duffy's signature collection of layered carpets.

In an effort to seamlessly blend old and new, McGeehan reclad the exterior in a lime-washed brick and replaced the faux columns holding up the entrance portico with proper nineteenth-century cast-iron examples he found in London and had shipped back. Inside, McGeehan has mixed Duffy's collection of early Provincetown paintings with English antiques, Moroccan and Persian rugs, and Chinese window screens. "My challenge is always to fit as many of Robert's things into his homes and make it work." The octagonal living room contains nine rugs layered on the floor under the original round spherules that dot the circular ceiling. "Whenever someone dies in my family I inherit rugs," says Robert.

The pool house was inspired by the original octagonal folly and now serves as an additional guest room. Duffy reports, "The house is very alive . . . filled to the brim with houseguests like an old-fashioned English weekend in the country. My houses are always made for my houseguests, with a flow that is people friendly."

A croquet court and the train tracks for Vincent Astor's miniature steam engine were originally on the grounds of the Tea House. They speak to a sense of earlier grandeur and history that now have receded into local Rhinebeck lore. Today, this much lived-in family home represents a new chapter in the history of the Ferncliff estate.

**ABOVE AND LEFT** The octagonal folly serving as the pool and guest pavilion was built with a nod to the original Tea House. Richard McGeehan selected antique marble tiles for the floor and a large tole chandelier with hundreds of porcelain flowers. **RIGHT** The train causeway that crosses Astor Cove was constructed in the 1850s.

# IN REMEMBRANCE OF LOST HOUSES

*Memento Mori: the theory and practice of reflection on the transient nature of earthly goods.* The scope of this book would not be complete without mention of Livingston homes that are no longer extant. The houses illustrated in these archival photographs, drawings, and paintings sadly have been destroyed. Today, conservation and preservation have become crucial to protecting our country's architectural patrimony. In the case of the Hudson Valley, this heightened attention is the result of the work implemented by many organizations, in particular, Hudson River Heritage, established in 1973, and the 1979 designation by the National Park Service of the Sixteen Mile District and the Clermont Estates Historic District. In addition, in 1990, the Hudson River National Historic Landmark District was created by the secretary of the interior, and in 1995, The Estates District within the Scenic Areas of Statewide Significance was designated by the New York State secretary of state. Partner organizations helping to fulfill this mission include planning and zoning leadership in Rhinebeck and Red Hook; the New York State Office of Parks, Recreation and Historic Preservation; Hudson River Greenway; Hudson River Valley National Heritage Area; Scenic Hudson; and Winnakee Land Trust.

**KIP-BEEKMAN-LIVINGSTON HOUSE 1698**
Built by Hendrick Kip on land acquired from Chief Ankony. President Franklin Roosevelt based the design of the Rhinebeck Post Office on this house, which burned in 1909.

**LIVINGSTON MANOR 1699**
This painting is thought to be a depiction of the manor house built by Robert Livingston, the First Lord, at the head of Roeliff Jansen Kill. The manor was dismantled in 1800.

**HENRY LIVINGSTON, SR., HOUSE 1743**
Built in Poughkeepsie by the son of Gilbert Livingston, the house later became the site of the Phoenix Horseshoe Company in 1870. The structure was razed in 1910.

**LOCUST GROVE 1771**
Built by Henry Livingston, Jr., on his father's property in Poughkeepsie. Henry is credited with writing the famous poem *A Visit from St. Nicholas* in 1805. Abandoned in 1830.

**THE HERMITAGE 1773**
Built by Peter R. Livingston originally as a one-story dwelling. Located in the Town of Livingston, it was bulldozed by owner Margaret Rockefeller in 1982.

**JOHN LIVINGSTON HOUSE 1775**
Before building Oak Hill, John built this house in the eponymously named hamlet of Johnstown, later named Livingston. Demolished in the mid-twentieth century.

**LINWOOD 1790**
The Federal house was built in Rhinebeck by Dr. Thomas Tillotson and his wife Margaret Livingston. In 1883, owner Jacob Ruppert had it razed to build his own house.

**NEW CLERMONT 1793**
Built by Robert "The Chancellor" Livingston, upon his return from Paris where he had served as the American ambassador. The interiors were decorated with murals by his grandson Montgomery Livingston. It later was renamed Idele in 1858 by the Clarkson sisters, and Arryl House in 1906 when owned by John Henry Livingston. Arryl House burned in 1909.

**PARNDON 1794**
Built by Henry Gilbert Livingston and sold to Jasper Parsons in 1795. Located in what is now Tivoli Bays, it was later called Eglington and Wilderkill. Demolished in 1909.

**MASSENA 1797**
John R. Livingston built his home in Barrytown using the plans of French engineer Marc Isambard Brunel, which loosely followed those of the Château de Beaumarchais. The house's name was given in honor of Napoleon's Marshal André Masséna. The house was greatly enlarged in 1860 by owner John Aspinwall. A subsequent house was built on this site in 1886.

**ALMONT 1797**
Built in Red Hook and named The Meadows by John Armstrong, who later built Rokeby. In 1813 it was renamed Almont by owner Robert Swift Livingston. Burned in 1877.

**MONCRIEF LIVINGSTON HOUSE 1798**
Built on land inherited from his grandfather Robert Livingston, Third Lord of Livingston Manor, the house burned in the 1920s.

**THE HILL 1799**
Attributed to architect Pierre Pharoux, the house was built in Linlithgo for Henry Walter Livingston, who had grown up at Teviotdale. It was destroyed by arson in 1972.

**ELLERSLIE 1814**
Built for Maturin and Mary Livingston using designs attributed to Benjamin Latrobe. The Tudor house designed by Richard Morris Hunt for Levi P. Morton replaced it in 1877.

**WAYSIDE 1820**
John Armstrong moved into his son Henry's house in Red Hook after selling Rokeby to his daughter Margaret and son-in-law William Backhouse Astor, Sr. Demolished.

**WRONGSIDE 1824**
Built for Charles Croghan and wife Angelica, who had grown up at Massena. Named for its location on the west side of the river, across from Rokeby, it recently burned.

**CRUGER ISLAND 1841**
Built by John Church Cruger and his wife, Euphemia Van Rensselaer, after drawings by A. J. Davis. Mayan sculptures were once placed on the property. Demolished in 1921.

**LEACOTE 1848**
Built by William Pratt Wainwright and his wife Cornelia Tillotson as The Meadows. It was purchased and renamed Leacote in 1875 by Douglas Merritt. Burned in 1977.

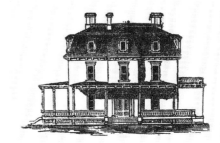

**HOPELAND 1864**
Built for Major Rawlins Lowndes and Gertrude Livingston by Calvert Vaux, who designed The Point. Enlarged by owner Robert P. Huntington in 1907 and demolished in the 1950s.

# NOTES

Unless otherwise stated, all quotations are from personal interviews and correspondence with the author.

**PAGE 9:** "The power of perpetuating . . ." Edmund Burke, J.C.D. Clark, ed., *Reflections on the Revolution in France: A Critical Edition*, (Palo Alto, CA: Stanford University Press, 2001).

**PAGE 13:** "There was not one . . ." Julia Delafield, *Biographies of Francis Lewis and Morgan Lewis*, vol. 1 (New York: Anson D. F. Randolph & Company, 1877), 193.

**PAGE 18:** "The first summer that young Robert . . ." Julia Delafield, *Biographies of Francis Lewis and Morgan Lewis*, vol. 1 (New York: Anson D. F. Randolph & Company, 1877), 122. "You are the cordial drop . . ." Letter from Robert Livingston to his wife, Margaret Beekman, Livingston Family Papers, Manuscripts and Archives Division, The New York Public Library.

**PAGE 21:** "He marked the epoch . . ." Thomas Streatfeild Clarkson, *A Biographical History of Clermont, or Livingston Manor, Before and During the War for Independence* (Clermont, NY: privately published, 1859), 24. "Washington admired the place . . ." Letter from Margaret Beekman to her son Robert, Livingston Family Papers, Manuscripts and Archives Division, The New York Public Library. "not pastry nor like the Scottish . . ." Harold Donaldson Eberlein, *The Manors and Historic Homes of the Hudson Valley* (Philadelphia: J. P. Lippincott, 1924), 78.

**PAGE 22:** "He was sufficiently contented . . ." George Dangerfield, *Chancellor Robert R. Livingston of New York, 1746–1813* (New York: Harcourt, Brace and Company, 1960), 188.

**PAGE 25:** "prostrated themselves and besought . . ." Alice Crary Sutcliffe, *Robert Fulton and The Clermont* (New York: The Century Co., 1909), 208.

**PAGE 26:** "imagination was that . . ."; "being hung with French . . ."; "Byronic detachment." George Dangerfield, *Chancellor Robert R. Livingston of New York, 1746–1813* (New York: Harcourt, Brace and Company, 1960), 187, 4, 193. "set on great . . ." Edwin Brockholst Livingston, *The Livingstons of Livingston Manor* (New York: The Knickerbocker Press, 1910), 481; "level or gently . . ." Andrew Jackson Downing, *A Treatise on the Theory and Practice of Landscape Gardening* (New York: A. O. Moore & Co., 1859, 27–8. "although politically the strictest . . ." John Henry Livingston, *The Livingston Manor* (Privately published, 1910), 37.

**PAGE 27:** "Cozen [sic] Robert is . . ." Letter from Margaret Beekman to a family member, Livingston Family Papers, Manuscripts and Archives Division, The New York Public Library. "delightful painting room . . ." Montgomery Livingston Papers, James D. Livingston Library, Germantown, New York, 5. "I'll never forget . . ." Allene G. Hatch, *Real Pearls and Darned Stockings: Tales of the Hudson Valley* (Privately published, 2011), 5.

**PAGE 33:** "distributing provisions . . ." Letter from Alida Schuyler Livingston to her husband, Robert, Livingston Family Papers, Franklin D. Roosevelt Presidential Library, Hyde Park, New York.

**PAGE 44:** "strong affection . . ." Kirkpatrick Sale, *The Fire of His Genius: Robert Fulton and the American Dream* (New York: Simon & Schuster, 2001), 65.

**PAGES 46-47:** "what I considered . . ."; "I did take" Peter Johnson, "Teviotdale: Designer's Eighteenth-Century Home in Upstate New York," *Architectural Digest*, June 1983, 126.

**PAGE 53:** "beautiful view . . ." Henry Gilbert Livingston quoted in Helen Wilkinson Reynolds, *Dutchess County Doorways and Other Examples of Period Work in Wood 1730–1830* (New York: William Farquhar Payson, 1931), 153.

**PAGES 60-61:** "In the story of the house . . ."; "have maintained it . . ." Helen Wilkinson Reynolds, *Dutchess County Doorways and Other Examples of Period Work in Wood 1730–1830* (New York: William Farquhar Payson, 1931), 159–60.

**PAGE 67:** "We can trace . . ." Jamie James, "Family Romances," *Connoisseur*, December 1988, 93.

**PAGE 76:** "the dignified . . ."; "Moral simplicity." Thomas Streatfeild Clarkson, *A Biographical History of Clermont, or Livingston Manor, Before and During the War for Independence* (Clermont, New York: Privately published, 1869), 259.

**PAGE 83:** "God had given him . . ." Louise Livingston Hunt, *Memoir of Mrs. Edward Livingston: With Letters Hitherto Unpublished* (New York: Harper & Brothers, Franklin Square, 1886), 41.

**PAGE 84:** "the beau ideal . . ." Pierre Munroe Irving, ed., *The Life and Letters of Washington Irving* (New York: G. P. Putnam's Sons, 1869), 76. "a woman of rare . . ." Thomas Streatfeild Clarkson, *A Biographical History of Clermont, or Livingston Manor, Before and During the War for Independence* (Clermont, New York: Privately published, 1869), 251.

**PAGE 86:** "Her friends . . ." Thomas Streatfeild Clarkson, *A Biographical History of Clermont, or Livingston Manor, Before and During the War for Independence* (Clermont, New York: Privately published, 1859), 254.

**PAGE 91:** "architectural composer." William Harvey Pierson, *American Buildings and Their Architects: Technology and the Picturesque* (New York: Doubleday, 1978), 282. "second as it is . . ." Jacquetta M. Haley, *Pleasure Grounds: Andrew Jackson Downing and Montgomery Place* (New York: Sleepy Hollow Press, 1988), 44.

**PAGE 92:** "Whether the charm . . ." Andrew Jackson Downing, *The Horticulturist and Journal of Rural Art and Rural Taste*, October 1854, 47.

**PAGE 103:** "is a farm superior . . ." Letter from General John Armstrong, Jr., to Rufus King, 1798, General John Armstrong Collection, The Patricia D. Klingenstein Library, The New-York Historical Society. "Alida enjoyed . . ."; "was presented . . ." William Astor Chanler, Jr., Typescript biography of John Armstrong, Patricia D. Klingenstein Library, The New-York Historical Society, 5, 7.

**PAGE 107:** "future lay . . ." William Astor Chanler, Jr., Typescript biography of John Armstrong, Patricia D. Klingenstein Library, The New-York Historical Society, 4.

**PAGE 110:** "genteel ladies . . ." William Astor Chanler, Jr., Typescript biography of John Armstrong, Patricia D. Klingenstein Library, The New-York Historical Society, 14.

**PAGE 114:** "monumental disputes . . ." Lately Thomas, *A Pride of Lions: The Astor Orphans* (New York: William Morrow & Co., 1971), 91. "Miss Chanler . . ." Margaret Chanler Aldrich, *Family Vista: The Memoirs of Margaret Chanler Aldrich* (New York: William-Frederick Press, 1958), 88. "the most promising . . ." Margaret Chanler, *Roman Spring: Memoirs by Mrs. Winthrop Chanler* (Boston: Little, Brown, and Company, 1934), 242. "The House of Fantasy . . ."; "with a head . . ." "Artist Chanler Paints These Things from Life," *The Sun* (New York), July 28, 1912.

**PAGE 115:** "Well into this generation . . ."; "cut about a dozen . . ." Margaret Chanler Aldrich, *Family Vista: The Memoirs of Margaret Chanler Aldrich* (New York: The William-Frederick Press, 1958), 11, 84.

**PAGE 120:** "thought it the consummation . . ." Robert Donaldson's words as quoted in Jean Bradley Anderson, *Carolinian on the Hudson, The Life of Robert Donaldson* (Raleigh, NC: The Historic Preservation Foundation of North Carolina, 1996), 163.

**PAGE 123:** "elegant and commodious"; "one to be glazed . . ." Robert Donaldson's words quoted in Jean Bradley Anderson, *Carolinian on the Hudson, The Life of Robert Donaldson* (Raleigh, NC: The Historic Preservation Foundation of North Carolina, 1996), 239, 240.

**PAGE 126:** "easily the most . . ."; "When a writer . . ." Gore Vidal, *Palimpsest: A Memoir* (New York: Random House, 1995), 243–44. "Your Lady . . ." Richard Hampton Jenrette, *More Adventures with Old Houses: The Edgewater Experience* (New York: Classical American Homes Preservation Trust, 2009), 24.

**PAGE 131:** "he wouldn't be able . . ." Susan Gillotti, *Women of Privilege: 100 Years of Love and Loss in a Family of the Hudson River Valley* (Chicago: Chicago Review Press, 2013), 30.

**PAGE 133:** "to read after . . ." Susan Gillotti, *Women of Privilege: 100 Years of Love and Loss in a Family of the Hudson River Valley* (Chicago: Academy Chicago Publishers, 2013), 9.

**PAGE 150:** "The great rambling . . ." Thomas Wolfe, *Of Time and the River* (New York: Charles Scribner's Sons, 1935), 556. "as a child . . ." Julia Olin's words quoted in Harold Donaldson Eberlein and Cortlandt Van Dyke Hubbard, *Historic Houses of The Hudson Valley* (New York: Dover Publications, Inc.), 84.

**PAGES 150-51:** "A deep cut . . ." Private Collection.

**PAGE 151:** "Holy code of prunes . . ." Julie Chanler, *From Gaslight to Dawn: An Autobiography* (New York: Pacific Printing Company, 1956), 40.

**PAGE 154:** "In June 1942 . . ." Olin Dows, *Franklin Roosevelt at Hyde Park* (New York: American Artists Group, 1949), 154.

**PAGE 162:** "one of the loveliest . . ." Frank Hasbrouck, *The History of Dutchess County* (Poughkeepsie, NY: S. A. Matthieu, 1909), 210.

**PAGE 164:** "You're really influenced . . ." Brice Marden's words quoted in Ted Loos, "A Subtle Sense of Place," Arts and Design section, *New York Times*, October 29, 2006, 1.

**PAGE 172:** "consists of a collection . . ." Hudson River National Historic Landmark District, application form, 1989.

**PAGE 178:** "the home didn't . . ." Facsimile of a letter from Eugene A. Livingston to Montgomery Livingston, September 19, 1844, James D. Livingston Library, Germantown, New York.

**PAGE 194:** "Polly, dear . . ." Sara Roosevelt's words quoted in Geoffrey C. Ward, *Closest Companion: The Unknown Story of the Intimate Friendship Between Franklin Roosevelt and Margaret Suckley* (New York: Simon & Schuster), 20.

**PAGES 194 AND 197:** "Driving home . . ." Eleanor Roosevelt, "My Day," syndicated newspaper column, Hyde Park, New York, July 1949.

**PAGE 210:** "Of course people . . ." Arthur Suckley's words quoted in Allene G. Hatch, *Real Pearls and Darned Stockings: Tales of the Hudson Valley* (Privately published, 2011), 56.

**PAGE 214:** "It's been a family trait . . ." Margaret Suckley's words quoted in Jan Geborsam, "More River Estates May Become Public Preserves," *Poughkeepsie Journal*, November 13, 1983, 3B.

**PAGE 217:** "step in and enjoy . . ." Robert H. Boyle, "Step In and Enjoy the Turmoil," *Sports Illustrated*, June 13, 1977, 81. "a large booming . . ." Gore Vidal, *Palimpsest: A Memoir* (New York: Random House, 1995), 258. "the face of . . ." Lately Thomas, *A Pride of Lions: The Astor Orphans, The Chanler Chronicle* (The University of Virginia: W. Morrow, 1971), 181.

**PAGE 221:** "What we mean . . ." A. J. Downing, *The Architecture of Country Houses: Including Designs for Cottages, Farms, and Villas* (New York: D. Appleton & Co. 1850), 257.

**PAGES 222-23:** "A well-balanced . . ."; (caption) "The hall . . ." Calvert Vaux, *Villas and Cottages: The Great Architectural Style-Book of the Hudson River School* (New York: Harper & Brothers, 1857), 51, 308.

**PAGE 252:** "My brother . . ." Eleanor Roosevelt, *This is My Story* (New York: Harper & Brothers, 1937), 37. "The house looks . . ." Eleanor Roosevelt, "My Day," syndicated newspaper column, Hyde Park, New York, August 10, 1940.

**PAGE 254:** "Money brings me . . ." John Jacob Astor III's words quoted in Eric Homberger, *Mrs. Astor's New York: Money and the Social Power in a Gilded Age* (New Haven, CT: Yale University Press, 2002), xiv. "so lavishly improved . . ." James H. Smith, *The History of Duchess County 1683–1882* (Syracuse, NY: D. Mason & Co., 1882), 280.

**PAGE 256:** "kept in the most perfect . . ." James H. Smith, *The History of Dutchess County 1683–1882* (Syracuse, New York: D. Mason & Co., 1882), 280. "Lewis Livingston . . ." *Rhinebeck Advocate*, 1876. "Once when a guest . . ." Gore Vidal, *Palimpsest: A Memoir* (New York: Random House, 1995), 240. "the demands . . ." Serge Obolensky, *One Man in His Time, The Memoirs of Serge Obolensky* (New York: McDowell, Obolensky, 1958), 269.

**PAGE 257:** "To give him . . ." Gore Vidal, *Palimpsest: A Memoir* (New York: Random House, 1995), 241. "no egg served . . ." St. Regis Hotel menu, 1930s.

**PAGE 278:** "to take chances . . ." Joan Davidson, J. M. Kaplan Fund Annual Report 2017.

**PAGE 291:** "The Upper Ten . . ." Julia Delafield, *Biographies of Francis Lewis and Morgan Lewis*, vol. 1 (New York: Anson D. F. Randolph & Company, 1877), 229. "All my life I . . ." Ward McAllister, *Society as I Have Found It* (New York: Cassell Publishing Company, 1890), 139.

**PAGE 304:** "the fragrance of the river . . ." Thomas Wolfe, *Of Time and the River* (New York: Charles Scribner's Sons, 1935), 539. "a little bit of heaven . . ."; "Swells . . ." Thomas Wolfe, *The Letters of Thomas Wolfe*, edited by Elizabeth Nowell (New York: Charles Scribner's Sons, 1956), 124, 82. "Didn't Linwood . . ." Henry James, *A Small Boy and Others* (New York: Charles Scribner's Sons, 1913), 181.

**PAGE 307:** "Where he outdid himself . . ."; "a life of . . ."; "the oldest . . ." Private Collection. "God only knows . . ." Cynthia Owen Philip, "Olin Dows, 1904–1981," Pamphlet from Museum of Rhinebeck History, Rhinebeck, New York, 1998. "To the mystification . . ." Gore Vidal, *Palimpsest: A Memoir* (New York: Random House, 1995), 263. "horrified that . . ." Rena Corey, "Thomas Wolfe and the Hudson River Aristocracy," *Hudson Valley Magazine*, July 1985, 30. "How many times . . ."; "Such a pity . . ." Private Collection. "And above all . . ."; "a dream house . . ." Thomas Wolfe, *Of Time and the River* (New York: Charles Scribner's Sons, 1935), 507, 515.

**PAGE 310:** "was a slender . . ." Gore Vidal, *Palimpsest: A Memoir* (New York: Random House, 1995), 240.

**PAGE 311:** "Isn't life . . ."; "the terribly attractive . . ."; "an exotic creature . . ." Serge Obolensky, *One Man in His Time, The Memoirs of Serge Obolensky* (New York: McDowell, Obolensky, 1958), 269. "She had also . . ." Gore Vidal, *Palimpsest: A Memoir* (New York: Random House, 1995), 273. "to help in case . . ." Allene G. Hatch, *Real Pearls and Darned Stockings: Tales of the Hudson Valley* (Privately published, 2011), 104.

**PAGE 318:** "He was the . . ." Julie Chanler, *From Gaslight to Dawn: An Autobiography* (New York: Pacific Printing Company, 1956), 264. "Lewis Stuyvesant Chanler, Sr. . . ." Obituary, *Poughkeepsie New Yorker*, February 1942.

# ACKNOWLEDGMENTS

TODAY, THE COMPLEXITY OF A PROJECT CAN BE MEASURED by the number of emails necessary to bring a book to publication. For mine, over eight thousand were exchanged with many who saw the subject's benefit. Two people who did not email me during this time were my son, Elio, and my partner, Joe Versace, who opted for the telephone urging me to come home. Thank you both for your patience and support (and typing) while I immersed myself in the Livingston family's history.

My Rizzoli editorial team was spearheaded by Sandy Gilbert Freidus, editor extraordinaire. I am impressed and inspired by her indefatigable energy, experience, and knowledge. When told I could call her at four in the morning, she meant it. Our relationship is one that instilled in me the optimism that bibliophiles still exist.

My friend David Byars went beyond the parameters of my expectations with his spectacular design and elevated visual sensibility. His knowledge of the history of the families and homes addressed in these pages provided many hilarious moments of dialogue.

Deborah Gardner was relentlessly committed to and crucial in the passing of a fine-tooth comb through the text's many passes. Certainly, she has earned an honorary degree on the topics covered while contributing great bonhomie during the process.

I thank Stephanie Salomon and Elizabeth Smith for their eagle eyes and impressive command of the English language.

Rizzoli's publisher Charles Miers has my utmost appreciation for believing in this project. The company's iconic former Fifth Avenue bookstore contributed to my obsession with books while growing up in Manhattan—so working together on this book project has held special significance for me.

I would like to thank John Winthrop "Wint" Aldrich for his insightful foreword and for providing his laser-sharp observations based on a combination of research, inquiry, and experience. That the patrimony of the region is in such respectable shape is due to his early work, along with Richard Crowley, in the formation of Hudson River Heritage and the Sixteen-Mile Historic District, as well as his involvement in the Historic American Buildings Survey that documented structures of importance in the region during the 1970s.

I appreciate the generosity of the homeowners, who opened their houses for me to photograph and look through their archives. Thank you for allowing me to interview you about your experiences as well as the historic Livingston thread that runs through the region.

My thanks to the wonderful team at Clermont, including Emily Robinson and Geoff Benton, and site manager Susan Boudreau. And thanks to Pam Malcolm, manager of Staatsburgh State Historic Site, for reopening the house's doors after we had completed photography and allowing us to run up to the roof to capture the mind-blowing sunset; Gregory Sokaris, executive director of Wilderstein Historic Site, who treated me to a visit of Margaret Suckley's bedroom; Amy Huston, who gave permission to photograph Montgomery Place; and Linda Cooper, for putting me in touch with Christopher Steber, public relations coordinator for New York State Parks, Recreation and Historic Preservation–Taconic Region.

In-depth research calls for librarians who are prepared to respond to unfamiliar requests. The following people made contributions toward these efforts: Claudine Klose of the Egbert Benson Historical Society in Red Hook and Joe Gatti at the Town of Livingston History Barn; Mike Frazier and Nancy Kelly at the Rhinebeck Library, who provided essential confirmation regarding several complex questions; Mark Boonshoft and Thomas Lannon at the Brooke Russell Astor Reading Room for Rare Books and Manuscripts at The New York Public Library, who lent research guidance and shared pertinent material including the George Bancroft transcripts of the Livingston papers, Janet Livingston Montgomery's memoirs, and letters in Robert "The Chancellor" Livingston's hand; Pamela Casey and Nicole Richard at the Avery Architectural and Fine Arts Library at Columbia University, who shared materials on Stanford White, including his personal letters and A. J. Davis's watercolors; Jill Reichenbach, who assisted with Livingston materials at the Patricia D. Klingenstein Library at the New-York Historical Society; at the Franklin D. Roosevelt Presidential Library in Hyde Park, archivist Christian Belena, who guided me to the most poignant seventeenth-century correspondence between Alida and Robert Livingston; and, in my own backyard, The James D. Livingston Library at Clermont Cottage, which offered a multitude of books on the family's history.

Emily Majer, Red Hook's town historian, shared her substantial research on Livingston homes in the area. Ray Armater made a significant contribution to the narratives of Wilderstein and Montgomery Place. Conrad Hanson not only invited me to join the Friends of Clermont but also shared his insightful information on the region. Clermont's executive director Jennifer Hemmerlein generously crafted grant applications to expand research.

A heartfelt thanks to Allene "Squeaky" Hatch—what an amazing privilege to hear your stories! I would also like to thank Veronique Firkusny, introduced to me by Marianne Thorsen, for sharing your reminiscences about the Dowses and Rhinebeck; and the Reverend Canon Elliott Lindsley, formerly at St. Paul's Church in Tivoli, and his wife, Barbara, for sharing illuminating tales of the Livingston family at memorable lunches in Millbrook.

Additional assistance was provided by numerous people living in the Hudson River Valley including Lauren Bailey, Nancy Beckham, Joshua Bronte, Carey Cahill, Heather Croner, Tyler Drosdeck, Jeremy Joyce, Mother Mark, Pat Melleby, Michael Pelletier, Brian Welsh, and Margize Howell, co-president of Classical American Homes Preservation Trust.

The lion's share of the book's post-production work is due to Frank Carbonari's technical expertise. Thanks go to James Senzer for his post-production work on the Chiddingstone chapter, and to Pablo Cubarle for helping produce the beautiful endpapers.

Thank you to my amazing assistants Tyler Kufs, Paul Strouse, Erik Swain, Craig Rockwell, and Desmond Reich during the shoots.

And finally my profound thanks to Melody Brynner, my dream agent at Art Department, who works with Kat Kelly and Nina Mouritzen in assisting me with all the support necessary to fulfill my professional obligations.

—PIETER ESTERSOHN

CASE COVER The Livingston shield and crest from John Henry Livingston's early-
twentieth-century bookplate. FRONT ENDPAPERS Portraits of Livingston family members;
The bookplate from Robert "The Chancellor" Livingston's copy of his 1809 volume
on animal husbandry. BACK ENDPAPERS A 1799 copy of the Crown Patent establishing
the Land Grant for the Manor of Livingston; Portraits of Livingston family members.

## CREDITS

**PAGE 10:** Photograph of Sylvania, Collection of John Winthrop Aldrich.

**PAGE 11:** Photograph of Steen Valetje, Collection of John Winthrop Aldrich.

**PAGE 18:** Engraving of a Clermont ram, from Robert R. Livingston, *Essay on Sheep* (T. and J. Swords, 1809), Collection of Victor Cornelius.

**PAGE 61:** Photograph of Olin Dows painting the drawing room at Callendar House, Dows Collection, Hudson River Heritage, Rhinebeck, New York.

**PAGE 78:** Watercolor of the view from Wildercliff by A. J. Davis, A. J. Davis Collection, Avery Architectural and Fine Arts Library, Columbia University.

**PAGE 93:** Photograph of a century plant and conservatory, Collection of Bard College, Montgomery Place Campus, Annandale-on-Hudson, New York.

**PAGE 131:** Photograph of Grasmere, Collection of Jonathan Mensch.

**PAGE 154:** Photograph of the wedding of Tracy Dows and Alice Olin, Dows Collection, Hudson River Heritage, Rhinebeck, New York.

**PAGE 179:** Eugene Augustus Livingston Family Photograph Collection, Patricia D. Klingenstein Library, The New-York Historical Society.

**PAGE 197:** Photograph of Steen Valetje (top) and drawing of Steen Valetje gatehouse (bottom), Private Collection.

**PAGE 214:** Photograph of a petroglyph, Collection of Wilderstein Historic Site, Rhinebeck, New York.

**PAGE 221:** Engraving of The Point from Calvert Vaux, *Villas and Cottages: The Great Architectural Style-Book of the Hudson River School* (New York: Harper & Brothers, 1857), 304.

**PAGE 227:** Gouache of Northwood, Private Collection.

**PAGE 251:** Photograph of Oak Lawn, Collection of Franklin D. Roosevelt Presidential Library, Hyde Park, New York.

**PAGE 257:** Photographs of Ferncliff (top) and Ferncliff Casino facade and pool (middle and bottom), Private Collection.

**PAGE 304:** Photograph of Olin Dows painting at Foxhollow Farm, Dows Collection, Hudson River Heritage, Rhinebeck, New York.

**PAGE 305:** Photograph of Foxhollow Farm's terrace, Rhinebeck Historical Society, Rhinebeck, New York.

**PAGES 332-33:** Archival photographs, drawings, and paintings of Livingston houses: Kip-Beekman-Livingston House; Linwood; Wayside: Rhinebeck Historical Society, Rhinebeck, New York. Livingston Manor: Private Collection of Susan Livingston.

Henry Livingston, Sr., House; Locust Grove: from HenryLivingston.com. The Hermitage; John Livingston House; Moncrief Livingston House: Livingston History Barn, Town of Livingston, New York. New Clermont: Clermont Historic Site, Germantown, New York. Parndon: Historic Red Hook, Red Hook, New York. Massena; Cruger Island; Leacote: Private Collection of John Winthrop Aldrich. Almont: Bard College Archives, Annandale-on-Hudson, New York. The Hill; Wrongside: Historic American Building Survey, Prints and Photography Division, Library of Congress, Washington, D. C. Ellerslie: from Benson J. Lossing, *The Hudson: From the Wilderness to the Sea* (Troy, NY: H. B. Nimes & Col, 1866). Hopeland: from Calvert Vaux, *Villas and Cottages: The Great Architectural Style-Book of the Hudson River School* (New York: Harper & Brothers, 1857), 296.

**CASEWRAP FRONT COVER:** John Henry Livingston's bookplate, New York State Office of Parks, Recreation, and Historic Preservation, New York.

**FRONT ENDPAPER:** Bookplate from Robert R. Livingston, *Essay on Sheep* (T. and J. Swords, 1809), Collection of Victor Cornelius.

**BACK ENDPAPER:** 1799 facsimile of the 1686 Livingston Manor land grant, Livingston Family Papers, Manuscripts and Archives Division, The New York Public Library.

First published in the United States of America in 2018
by Rizzoli International Publications, Inc.
300 Park Avenue South
New York, New York 10010
www.rizzoliusacom

2020 2021 2022/10 9 8 7 6 5 4 3
Printed in China
ISBN 13: 978-0-8478-6323-5
Library of Congress Control Number: 2018944544
Project Editor: Sandra Gilbert Freidus
Editorial Assistance: Deborah Gardner, Stephanie Salomon, Elizabeth Smith, Sara Pozefsky
Production: Kaija Markoe

ART DIRECTION AND DESIGN: DAVID BYARS

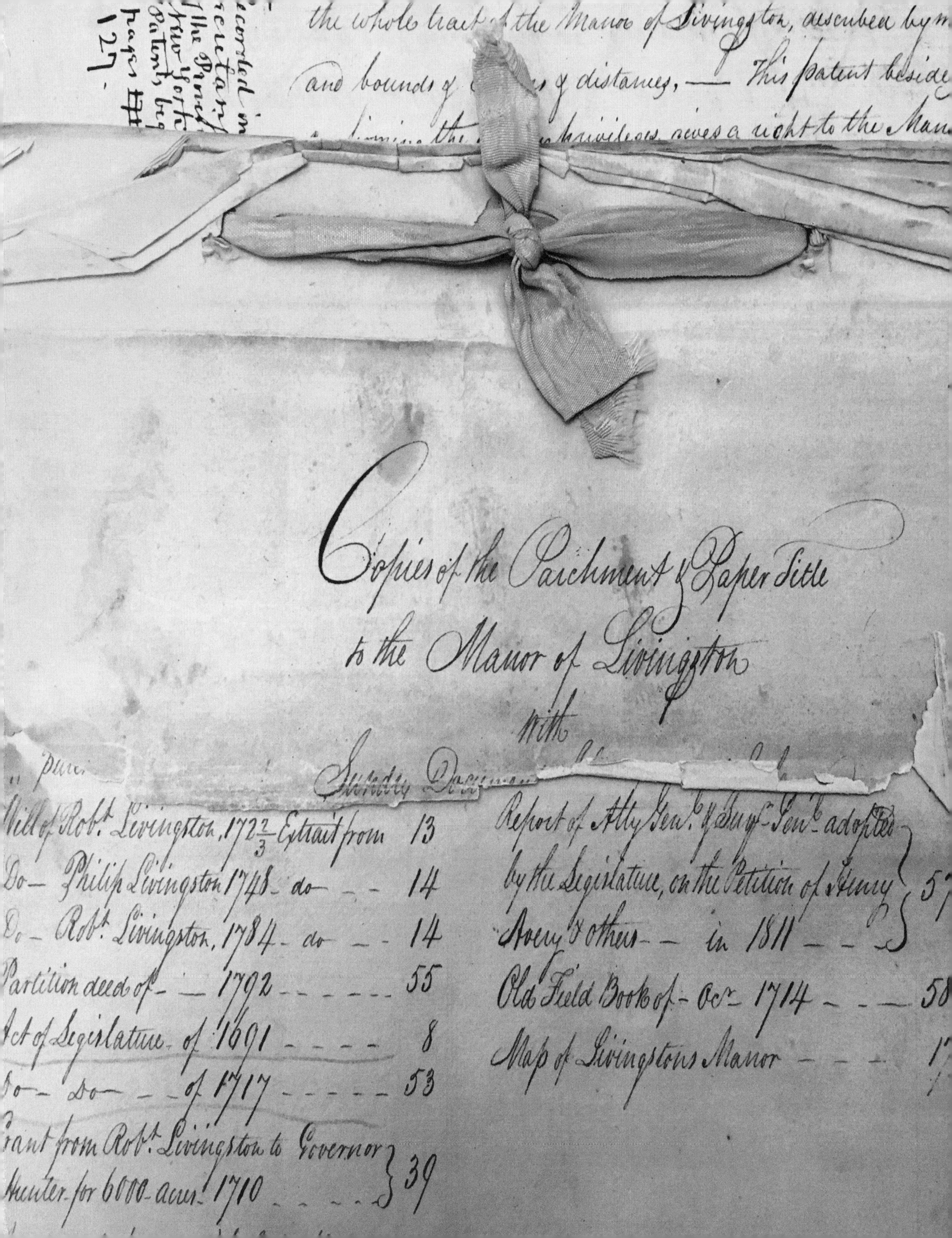

the whole tract of the Manor of Livingston, described by m[...]

and bounds of [...] & distances, —— This patent beside[s]

[...] giving the [...] privileges gives a right to the Man[...]

*Copies of the Parchment & Paper title*

*to the Manor of Livingston*

*with*

*Sundry Documents*

| | | | | |
|---|---|---|---|---|
| Will of Robt. Livingston, 1722/3 Extract from | 13 | Report of Atty Genl. & Surv. Senl. adopted | | |
| Do — Philip Livingston 1748 — do — | 14 | by the Legislature, on the Petition of Henry | | 5[1] |
| Do — Robt. Livingston, 1784 — do — | 14 | Avery & others — in 1811 — | | |
| Partition deed of — 1792 | 55 | Old Field Book of — Octr 1714 — | | 58 |
| Act of Legislature of 1691 | 8 | Map of Livingstons Manor — | | 1[...] |
| Do — Do — of 1717 | 53 | | | |
| Grant from Robt. Livingston to Governor Hunter for 6000 acres 1710 | 39 | | | |

[Left margin, vertical:]
recorded in [...] secretary [...] the Pend [...] New York, [...] Patent, [...] [...] 127.